KANRYO

KANRYO

JAPAN'S HIDDEN GOVERNMENT

by TADAHIDE IKUTA

translated by Hideo Yanai

ICG Muse, Inc.
New York, Tokyo, Osaka & London

Published by ICG Muse, Inc.
73 Spring Street, #206, New York, NY 10012.
2-7-20 Kita-Aoyama, Minato-ku, Tokyo 107-0061.

Distributed by Tuttle Shokai Inc.
2-7-20 Kita-Aoyama, Minato-ku, Tokyo 107-0061.

ISBN 4-925080-33-4

Originally published in 1995
by NHK Publishing, Tokyo.

First ICG Muse edition, 2000

CONTENTS

PREFACE TO THE ENGLISH EDITION

Drastic political change is taking place in Japan. Within the space of a single year there have been four prime ministers in succession: Miyazawa Kiichi, Hosokawa Morihiro, Hata Tsutomu, and Murayama Tomiichi. While it is impossible to predict what type of system Japanese politics will ultimately settle into, whether a two-party structure as in the United States or a multi-party rule as in Italy, one thing is certain: it will take a long time for the situation to settle down. Even political scientists and the most optimistic of politicians expect the present situation of short-lived administrations to last several more years. Others speculate it will take much longer for the confusion to subside.

Despite the political chaos and the revolving political leadership, the Japanese people have remained relatively calm. Why? Primarily, the Japanese have never expected much from politics, as exemplified in a popular Japanese expression, "economy first-rate, politics third-rate." A prominent Japanese business leader once commented that "the only thing politicians need to do is to stay out of trouble. They should concern themselves with nothing else."

However, there is a more important reason behind the general apathy in Japan toward the political ferment, and that is the fact that the country's higher-ranking bureaucrats, or *kanryo*, have held de facto control of the government for over eleven decades since the introduction of the Cabinet system of 1885. In theory, Japan is a parliamentary democracy; ostensibly, politicians are elected by the people to govern the country. In fact, bureaucrats are far more powerful than politicians.

Japanese tend to feel secure in the knowledge that the nation's "academically brilliant" bureaucrats control the government. Japan's bureaucrats include some of the brightest college graduates in the fields of law and economics. A career in the bureaucracy is considered an honorable profession and it involves rigorous training upon taking office. Moreover, these bureaucrats are much more serious about their work than politicians. The political upheaval has only served to strengthen the bureaucracy, leading some to say that Japan is run by a "dictatorship of bureaucrats." A number of bureaucrats have recently remarked that as long as politicians are in a state of disarray, bureaucrats have a responsibility to work harder than ever.

Political turmoil was triggered in August 1993 during the elections for the lower house seats of the Diet (the national legislative body) with the defeat of the Liberal Democratic Party (LDP), the ruling political party in Japan since 1955. As a consequence of these elections, the LDP now holds less than a majority of the seats in the House of Representatives. The biggest reason for the defeat of the LDP was due to the defection of nearly fifty LDP members into two new opposition factions. One of the most notable features of the LDP's long legacy of dominating Japanese politics had been the strong alliance that it had forged with the bureaucracy.

For more than a century Japanese bureaucracy has been instrumental in protecting and promoting industries such as manufacturing, finance, commerce, agriculture, forestry, and fisheries. For example, the Ministry of Finance has been responsible for insurance, finance, and the securities industries. The Ministry of International Trade and Industry (MITI) has fostered the automotive, consumer electric appliance, and machinery industries while regulating energy resources such as petroleum, natural gas and electrical power. Under the bureaucracy's protection and guidance, Japan's businesses have flourished, helping the nation become an economic power to be reckoned with. As a result of its astonishing postwar economic growth, Japan is now an industrial state with the world's second largest GNP.

However, though it has emerged as an economic superpower in the past decade, Japan's basic bureaucratic structure, geared toward the protection and promotion of industries, has not changed. Given the highly developed state of Japanese industry, a growing number of politicians, business executives, and scholars, both inside and outside of Japan, consider bureaucratic protection and promotion of industries to be no longer necessary. These critics, who are increasing in number, call for industry deregulation and a more consumer-oriented bureaucracy. Moreover, while continuing to respect the traditional authority of the kanryo, Japanese society too has been growing impatient with a rigid, inflexible bureaucratic system that has failed to adequately serve their needs. The bureaucracy itself shows signs of obsolescence.

Predictably, the bureaucracy, industry, and LDP politicians are not interested in joining the debate on reforming the Japanese government. Each government agency in Kasumigaseki (the district of Tokyo where the important government agencies are located and the name for the agencies and bureaucrats collectively), has developed and protected its own turf, including the various industries under its jurisdiction. The bureaucracy seeks to maintain, not abolish, the present system of public administration. Industry has been protected and promoted by the bureaucracy, and in turn, LDP politicians receive support, in the form of votes and money, from industry during election time. Dubbed the "Iron Triangle," these three groups—politicians, bureaucracy, and industry—through their strong relationships protect each other's interests. Japan's bureaucratic structure has become detached from economic reality.

One consequence of this rigid structure, for instance, is that while the apportionment of the national budget among government agencies ought to fluctuate as the Japanese economy changes, in recent years this apportionment has been virtually fixed. Even the Ministry of Finance, the agency responsible for creating the budget, can do little to resist the Iron Triangle. As Japanese businesses become increasingly international, opening the Japanese markets for the sale of foreign goods should be a natural consequence. However, because of strong opposition from the Iron Triangle this process too has foundered. As a result, prices of consumer goods in Japan are inordinately expensive compared to those in other industrial nations.

To put it plainly, the Iron Triangle has distorted the raison d'être of the bureaucracy. Bureaucrats are supposed to serve the people; in truth, the objective of Japan's bureaucrats is to protect the ties between politicians and industries that fall under their particular agency's jurisdiction. The bureaucrats have distorted their primary objective into a survival game that involves protecting their agency's turf and invading that of others. In Kasumigaseki, agencies compete with each other not for the public good but for self-interest. Some bureaucrats have diagnosed this dilemma as "system fatigue." Evidently, Japan's bureaucracy, once indispensable to the nation's economic development, now does more harm than good.

The end of the LDP's political reign in August 1993 was due as much to the rejection of the party by Japan's urban residents as to a power struggle among conservative politicians. The *sarariman* ("salaried man," or white-collar worker) contingent in particular has grown the most hostile towards the Iron Triangle, and it has ultimately directed its animosity towards the LDP. As election surveys indicate, in urban areas the LDP has been reduced to minority party status for quite some time. Though the LDP, at present, has regained power by forging a coalition with its former arch-enemy, the Social Democratic Party of Japan, it has largely lost the influence it previously took for granted.

Japanese politics is likely to continue through a series of confusing twists and turns, but I am certain that the politicians must heed the Japanese people's call for change. How will Japan's bureaucrats react to demands to reform administrative structure? As an investigative journalist, I have covered the Japanese bureaucracy for over ten years and have interviewed hundreds of bureaucrats and former bureaucrats. My overall impression from these encounters is that undoubtedly the bureaucracy as a whole will adamantly oppose deregulation and will resist the restructuring of the existing system with considerable vehemence. The opinions of those individual bureaucrats who openly recognize the need for improvement and strongly support reform initiatives, will, unfortunately, probably be ignored. The

Japanese bureaucracy is firmly entrenched in the principles of group organization and tends to suppress individual initiative.

By American standards, the administrative practices of the Japanese bureaucracy must seem incredible. In this book, I intend to describe how Japan's bureaucracy ticks, and to reveal, by means of specific examples, the attitude of the kanryo toward their work. If this book aids Western readers in understanding Japan a little better, my objective will have been fulfilled.

Notes on the Translation

This book, originally published in Japan in 1992, is the product of the author's decade-long coverage of the government agencies and the bureaucrats in Kasumigaseki. Parts of the book are based on magazine articles published in Japan between 1990 and 1992. Additional chapters that have been added for the Western reader not only provide needed background, but bring the account up to the present date.

All Japanese names, except those of the author and translator, are presented in Japanese order, that is, family name first and given name second (except in certain quotes).

PREFACE TO THE JAPANESE EDITION

When the Persian Gulf crisis was triggered by the Iraqi invasion of Kuwait in August of 1990, Japan's high-level government officials, particularly the director-generals and administrative vice-ministers, were thrown into a state of confusion. The bureaucracy was unable to respond effectively to U.S. demands for financial aid to support the military effort or to the proposal to dispatch Japan's Self Defense Forces to support the United Nations Peace Keeping Force. The bureaucrats were made painfully conscious that their system of government was incapable of dealing with change and drastically needed an overhaul.

Some months after the Persian Gulf crisis, I went to Kasumigaseki to interview a director-general of one of the ministries. When discussing the confusion in the bureaucracy, the director-general was at first logical and coherent. Then all of a sudden, he was at a loss for words. In exasperation, he blurted out: "I would never advise my child to become a public servant. I wager that there is no country that abuses its government officials as Japan does. Whenever we do something that we believe will truly benefit the Japanese people, special interest groups and vested-interest Diet members who oppose our propositions make totally unreasonable demands on us. If we don't listen to them, we could get fired. I have no hope whatsoever for Kasumigaseki. I will leave when my time comes. But I ask only one thing from all high-ranking officials: create a system that is truly accountable to the people, and let us move beyond petty bureaucratic interests." Shortly after this discussion, a Ministry of Foreign Affairs official confided in me: "I wonder if Japan will survive so much bureaucrat bashing. The only chance for Japan's officials to start over is to be receptive to criticism, keep an open mind and prepare for the future by instituting constructive, concrete changes in the system."

While the bureaucracy was still troubled by issues surrounding Japan's cooperation with the United Nations peacekeeping operations another shocking problem burst to the forefront. On the afternoon of December 5, 1990, Yamauchi Toyonori, the director-general of the Environment Agency's Planning and Coordination Bureau, hung himself in the bedroom of his suburban Tokyo home. He was discovered suspended by an electric cord from a ceiling beam and had written a suicide note on the back of one of his business cards. Addressed to his family, the note simply stated, "Thank you for everything." The next day, news of Yamauchi's suicide was taken up by the media. On that very day, I visited several government agencies, including the Ministry of Health and Welfare and the Environment Agency, to ask various officials for their comments on the suicide. Most were taciturn, but the sight of several visibly shaken officials told me that something about the news had hit home. It felt as though overnight Kasumigaseki had been covered with frost.

Indeed, widespread demoralization among top-level bureaucrats is a most alarming phenomenon, as indicated by the increasing number of officials who have quit their jobs. In the decade that I have been reporting on the government agencies, I have observed that Kasumigaseki seems to have changed significantly; discussion of important topics seems far less dynamic than it used to be, and it is now pervaded with an atmosphere of anxiousness, cynicism, and intolerance. Not only is Kasumigaseki's structure seriously flawed, but those who are running the system are in crisis. It may be safely said that the problems of the bureaucrats are more dangerous to the nation than to the system itself.

Although it is clear that the bureaucracy seriously needs restructuring, little has been done, and that inconsistently. Many bureaucrats themselves have begun to understand the necessity of reform. For example, Naito Masahisa, former director-general of the Basic

Industries Bureau of the Ministry of International Trade and Industry (MITI), has stated:

> High officials in various agencies have felt that postwar Japan did not have a sufficient perception of itself as a nation-state. The Persian Gulf crisis intensified that feeling. Kasumigaseki is losing ground while the private sector expands both at home and abroad. Interagency disputes are getting out of hand. Japan thus far has been led by the bureaucracy, but if present trends continue, I am afraid the bureaucracy will do more harm than good to the country.
>
> After the outbreak of the Persian Gulf crisis, we wondered if Kasumigaseki could keep running the country in the same manner. Bureaucrats, who to begin with had a lot in common with one another, now had an even stronger shared sense of mission to effectively respond to the political agenda.

Sakamoto Yoshihiro, former chief of the Machinery and Information Industries Bureau at MITI, has been quoted as saying: "MITI's role in industrial development is over. Now MITI has to decide what its functions should be in the context of Japan as a whole, not just Japanese industry." Such a remark by a MITI official would have been unthinkable a few years earlier, and Sakamoto seemed to have all of Kasumigaseki in mind, not just MITI. A councilor at the Ministry of Home Affairs stated: "I recommend restructuring the agencies. For instance, MITI and the Ministry of Agriculture, Forestry and Fisheries could be combined into a Ministry of Agriculture and Commerce, just as in the prewar era. We could also improve efficiency by merging the National Land Agency, the Ministry of Construction, and the Ministry of Home Affairs into one ministry."

The problem is, of course, that these opinions from bureaucrats do not automatically lead to immediate changes. First of all, strong resistance within Kasumigaseki itself would most certainly rise against reform measures. More importantly, politicians from both houses would not readily agree to reduce the number of Cabinet ministerial posts because these are among the most coveted political prizes.

A most pressing question for Japan's future then is, what forces will effect a change in the bureaucracy? Kasumigaseki must begin to take a good long look at itself. It is no wonder that when the structure of Japan's bureaucracy has remained basically unchanged since the introduction of the Cabinet system of 1885, it is inadequate for meeting the challenges of the coming generations. Just as the Soviet Union, arguably a bureaucratic paradise, had to face the problems of its government structure, so too, the system of government in Kasumigaseki is in turmoil, and must undergo a revolution. According to the economist Joseph A. Schumpeter, "The success of capitalism leads to its decline." If we apply Schumpeter's dictum to Japan's bureaucracy-led economic development, we see that it is time for the bureaucracy to step aside, and allow a new system to take over.

In this book, I examine why and how such a sense of crisis has developed in the bureaucracy. Since late 1990 the Japanese media has frequently reported on the setbacks and shortcomings of Kasumigaseki and on the growing number of high officials who quit and turn to the private sector. But conspicuously absent is a systematic examination of both the bureaucracy's structural problems and the call for reform. Thus, the focus of this book is on the bureaucrats' changing perception of themselves and their relationship to the outside world, the bureaucracy's interagency conflicts and power struggles, and the emerging internal and external initiatives to reform the bureaucracy.

Acknowledgments

Portions of this book have been adapted from such magazines as *Sentaku, Foresight,* and *Zaikai Tenbo,* with additions and corrections. I greatly appreciate the cooperation of the editorial staff at those magazines.

KANRYO

OVERVIEW OF THE BUREAUCRACY

Composition of the Bureaucracy

As of April 1992, the Japanese bureaucracy in the broader sense was composed of approximately 4,491,000 public officials at both the national and local levels. Of those government officials, approximately 1,167,000, or one in four, worked at the national level. National-level public officials may be grouped into four categories, according to the nature of their work:

1. Special Officials, numbering approximately 329,000. Examples include members of the Self-Defense Forces, members of the Diet, and judges.
2. Public Prosecutors, numbering approximately 2,000.
3. On-Site Officials, numbering approximately 327,000. Examples include postal service workers, postal savings system (PSS) employees, and the officials who manage the national forests.
4. Regular Officials, numbering approximately 509,000. This category consists primarily of administrators in the

national government, but it also includes professionals such as professors at national universities, doctors and nurses at national hospitals, and researchers at national research institutes. The lower levels of the bureaucracy are highly unionized.

The Elite of the Bureaucracy

It must be emphasized, however, that in this book the English words "bureaucracy" and "bureaucrat" are not used in the broad sense to refer to government officials in general; rather, they are used in a narrower sense to refer to the *kanryo*, that is, the elite class among the regular officials at the national level. The elite of the bureaucracy are those who graduated from prestigious universities and serve at such agencies as the Ministry of Foreign Affairs, the Ministry of Finance, the Ministry of International Trade and Industry (MITI), and the National Police Agency. Each government agency selects and recruits these elite career officials from among the successful candidates of the Level I Entrance Examination for the National Civil Service. (The Ministry of Foreign Affairs is one exception in that it administers a separate Diplomatic Service Examination of its own.) The annual cutthroat competition among government agencies to recruit the most capable individuals will be described later in greater detail.

There are approximately 18,000 of these elite bureaucrats who have passed the Level I Entrance Examination for the National Civil Service. While representing only 3.5 percent of all the national-level officials, the elite take virtually 100 percent of the highest positions attainable by officials in this category, that is, all administrative vice-minister and director-general, or bureau chief, positions. Minister and director positions are occupied by politicians, almost all of whom must be Diet members in accordance with Article 68 of the Constitution of Japan. The Japanese government is a parliamentary system whose Cabinet members are, generally speaking, legislators. Successful candidates from the other Entrance Examinations for the National Civil Service, such as Level II for college and junior college graduates, and Level III for high school graduates, have virtually no chance of becoming a director-general; odds of this happening would be less than once every ten years, and the event would attract great media attention. Very few of these non-elite, or non-career, regular officials rank higher than division chief or section chief.

In fact, as long as an elite bureaucrat does nothing unethical or illegal such as taking bribes, and does not criticize the establishment, he or she is assured, at the very least, of reaching the position of division chief, or section chief. The elite quickly move up the ranks of bureaucracy in a path nicknamed the "bullet train course"; meanwhile, their non-elite compatriots are routed to the "local train course." For example, elite-class bureaucrats at the Ministry of Finance usually become chiefs of local tax bureaus in the outlying prefectures by their late twenties, where their subordinates are mostly in their fifties. It is typical for elite-class officials to give orders to non-elite officials who are their parents' age.

The status accorded the elite bureaucrats has its roots in the Confucian influence upon Japan's traditional society. This is often described as a "vertical society," and understanding its structure is essential to understanding Japanese society today. Prior to the Meiji Restoration of 1868, the Japanese lived under a feudal system; they were divided into four classes beneath the emperor: samurai, farmer, craftsman, and merchant, in that order of official importance. This hierarchy established what was considered superior or inferior, and this "above and below" concept was extended to relations between the government and the people; the elderly and youth; client and vendor; and so on. Interestingly, this vertical structure was also responsible for forging the close links between members of "horizontal" groupings (i.e., people of the same "vertical" rank). Such links can be seen today in the tight bonds between university students or same-year entrants into the bureaucracy.

The government must be respected in a vertical society, and bureaucrats have assumed a supreme authority in their roles of administrative executors. Businesses have been relegated to a position in which they must respect the bureaucracy. This dominant role of the bureaucracy in Japanese society and business, and the hierarchical principles operating within the bureaucracy itself, are sometimes referred to collectively as "vertical administration." Japan's educational system further reflects this vertical organization; the University of Tokyo is considered the top school while the other universities are ranked below it in descending order. While the principles of a vertical society are gradually losing their hold on Japanese psychology, the process will take some time; bureaucrats still think of themselves as "the best" of the system and assume that society should trust them implicitly.

The Japanese people have historically looked upon the elite class with special reverence. When members of different occupational groups sit down together at a meeting, these elite bureaucrats, even the younger ones, are always given the best seats. Even presidents of major corporations such as Toyota and NEC must act as juniors, subordinate to the section chiefs or division chiefs of MITI no matter what their actual ages. Where kanryo are concerned, the Asian tradition of respecting one's elders is put aside. The Japanese media also grant bureaucrats special treatment. Though in recent years newspapers, weekly magazines, and television programs have been criticizing the way bureaucrats are running the government, these media rarely imply that bureaucrats are no longer necessary or that they do more harm than good to Japan. Most Japanese feel that although the bureaucracy has its problems, on the whole the elite bureaucrats are intelligent and industrious and no one else could do a better job. When comparing itself to bureaucrats, Japanese society tends to exhibit an inferiority complex.

Rebuilding the Economy

Emerging from the devastating defeat of World War II, Japan began the process of reconstructing its economy. Possessing few natural resources, Japan focused upon developing its export industries and building up its foreign currency reserves. With this foreign currency earned, Japan purchased minerals, petroleum, and other natural resources while enthusiastically introducing foreign technology. As its domestic industry developed, Japan's export industry grew internationally competitive. After initially gaining ground in heavy industries such as steel and shipbuilding, Japan next established itself in some of the world's most competitive manufacturing industries, including automobiles, semiconductors, construction machinery, and consumer electronics and electric appliances.

As a consequence of its industrial development, Japan has come to accumulate the largest foreign currency reserves in the world and has built an economy with a GNP second only to that of the United States. Its present situation is a far cry from the foreign currency shortages experienced for more than twenty years after the war. In 1993, Japan's foreign currency reserves amounted to $610.8 billion. On that basis, Japan has been the richest country in the world for three years in a row. What made Japan's spectacular growth possible? A number of economic causes are frequently cited. For example, petroleum and mineral resources had to be imported by sea in mass quantities, but then transport costs were lower than overland transport costs would have been. Japan reduced domestic transport costs by building industrial complexes on the coast. However, there are certainly other, more fundamental reasons underlying Japan's rapid economic development.

Probably the most significant contribution to Japan's spectacular economic growth was made by its vast, highly-educated, and hard-working labor force, both blue-collar workers and the *sarariman*. After the war, they persevered, year after year, under long work hours and poor living conditions. Motivated by the belief that only their companies could raise their living standards, they sacrificed their private lives for the sake of their employers. Japanese "company warriors" have demonstrated extreme loyalty to their companies as they fought with military-like discipline to prevail over competitors.

Factory workers not only performed their given jobs, but suggested ways to improve manufacturing processes. White-collar workers entertained clients after work hours and often came home to their families late at night. If assigned to overseas branch offices, they often went abroad alone, separated from their families. These employees have been the driving force behind the success of global giants like NEC, Toyota, Toshiba, Hitachi, Mitsubishi Heavy Industries, and Matsushita Electric (Panasonic).

The bureaucracy has played an equally great role in Japan's post-war economic growth by creating an environment conducive to business. As previously noted, responsibility for fostering particular types of industries is divided among agencies of the national government, with the Ministry of Finance and the Ministry of International Trade and Industry (MITI) playing important roles. In encouraging its respective industries, each agency has been motivated to cultivate its sphere of influence and thereby become indispensable within the government. If an industry under one agency's supervision failed to develop properly, the agency would render itself powerless and therefore obsolete. Throughout the postwar years and down to the present, each agency has sought to protect its influence in the government.

Agencies have a variety of useful protective measures at hand to achieve this end. An agency can protect its industries, and maintain its control over them, by building barriers against newcomers, both foreign and domestic, through its exclusive power to license. Another control measure an agency can use is industry subsidies, a matter of vested interest for both industry and agency. During the thirty-eight years of LDP political domination, bureaucrats and industry leaders worked earnestly to get as much in subsidies as possible for certain industries by lobbying Diet members and by sponsoring *zoku* legislators (legislators who are sympathetic to and well-connected to particular interest groups). A third device that Japan's government agencies use to keep control over its respective industries under their jurisdiction is the practice of "administrative guidance."

Administrative Guidance

In Japan, the term "administrative guidance" is used to refer to nonbinding recommendations by a national government agency to a private sector company or a local government. The company or local government does not have to obey administrative guidance because it carries with it no specific power of enforcement. But to avoid retaliation from a national agency and to keep a good relationship with the bureaucracy, a company or local government office usually complies.

If an agency's recommendations are ignored, retaliation may ensue in one of several ways. The agency might leak the name of the noncomplying company or local government to the media. Since in most cases administrative guidance is issued only after the agency has held lengthy discussions with the company or local government, disobeying it is considered tantamount to engaging in disruptive and anti-social behavior. A commercial organization thus exposed in the media would likely suffer financially from its damaged image among consumers. Or, the agency might practice the proverbial Japanese saying, "Take revenge in Nagasaki for a wrong done in Edo," that is, the agency might not retaliate right away, but would do so at a later time. The agency's bureaucrats might appear to look the other way when a company or local government disobeys administrative guidance, but eventually reprisal will come in some other field of public administration. Since Japan is a "Bureaucrats' Kingdom," the bureaucracy may choose to retaliate anywhere at any time.

However, these types of retaliatory measures may be losing their effectiveness as Japanese companies become more powerful and often do not necessarily see eye to eye with bureaucrats. Also, a growing faction in the media has become increasingly critical of bureaucrats, placing the very concept of administrative guidance under fire. Demands are increasing to abolish directives that are not backed by specific law.

If administrative guidance were altered or completely abolished, the influence of bureaucrats on Japanese society would diminish to a considerable degree. Bureaucrats become very anxious when they contemplate this prospect. A high-ranking Ministry of Health and Welfare official remarked: "I wonder if Japan would be able to function without a strong bureaucracy. Not only Japanese companies but the general public lack self-discipline and a sense of social responsibility. Japanese society as well as the economy would fall into total chaos if everyone were given total freedom."

As can be seen from the argument just quoted, bureaucrats would fiercely oppose any outside attempt to weaken their power. As a countermeasure to reform efforts, bureaucrats have expanded their licensing powers under the law. According to the Management and Coordination Agency, the number of licenses being issued by the Japanese government as a whole was 11,402 as of the end of March 1993, an increase of 13.4 percent over the number being issued ten years earlier.

Not surprisingly, economic agencies control the largest number of licenses. The breakdown of ministry licensing is as follows: MITI, 17.4

percent; Transport, 16.6 percent; Agriculture, Forestry and Fisheries, 12.5 percent; Finance, 12.2 percent; Health and Welfare, 10.7 percent; Construction, 8.0 percent; others, 17.1 percent. MITI ranks first largely because it has greater authority over public administration than other agencies and still controls an array of regulatory licenses on energy-related matters. On the other hand, because it has advocated deregulation, MITI imposes fewer regulations on big business than the other agencies impose on their industries. As a result, foreign companies may obtain licenses in MITI-supervised industries with relative ease. Exceptions include energy-related industries, such as electric power, natural gas, and petroleum refineries, and large retail franchises. On the deregulation of retail operations, MITI officials are quietly positive. But the Large-scale Retail Stores Law, a law written by MITI, has been thwarted by politicians representing small store owners who oppose any change. A MITI official commented that "the inability to deregulate retail is a real sore point."

Economic agencies other than MITI, however, are not as open-minded about deregulating industries under their influence and are extremely protective of their turf. For example, the Ministry of Construction, which is responsible for public works projects such as roads, bridges, and sewage systems, is hard-pressed to restructure the construction bidding system, an area increasingly coming under fire. For many of Japan's major construction projects the government's "designated competitive bidding" system differs from America's open bidding system. Under this system, Ministry of Construction bureaucrats evaluate the respective qualifications of construction companies and decide which companies should be allowed to bid. The selected companies then hold secret meetings among themselves to decide the winning bidder and set the price for the project. This practice, which is actually a form of collusion, is called *dango*, or "consultation." The winner gets a high price, and the cooperating companies share parts of the project.

Ministry of Construction bureaucrats, particularly the technical officials who administer the designated competitive bidding, claim that this system guarantees high-quality work on construction projects. They say they are concerned that if open bidding were allowed too much competition would ultimately cause construction companies to go out of business. Designated competitive bidding, then, has been defended as a method of ensuring smaller companies will have a chance at getting a contract. For these reasons, the ministry has prohibited foreign companies from participating in an open bidding system for government construction projects. Nevertheless, demands from the United States to open Japanese markets and recent public works-related scandals involving politicians and heads of local governments have led to cries for bidding reform. Concrete outcomes of such criticism include the introduction of a managed open bidding system in some projects and the establishment of a bidding supervision committee. But because these reform measures are seen as limited and superficial, they are expected to bring little change to the present situation.

An obvious question that might arise is why the ministry does not simply change the bidding system and introduce open competition. The reason most often given is that the Ministry of Construction, like the Ministry of Finance, the Ministry of Transport, the Ministry of Health and Welfare, and the Ministry of Agriculture, Forestry, and Fisheries, fears that the industries under its supervision will be thrown into confusion and thereby weakened. Like the bureaucracy, existing companies, too, seek to impede new competitors. In this respect bureaucracy and industry share common ground in their fear of rising foreign competition. Licensing, which is the major barrier obstructing foreign competition, is an entrenched practice in Japan. The variety and scope of business activities subject to licensing are growing year by year. However, there is another, less obvious, reason for the bureaucracy to continue resisting the introduction of open competition, and that is that it would jeopardize bureaucrats' prospects for post-retirement careers under the practice known as *amakudari*.

Descent from Heaven

Literally meaning "descent from heaven," the word *amakudari* is a metaphor originating in Japanese myth of the descent from heaven by deities to create and inhabit the Japanese archipelago. In contemporary parlance, *amakudari* refers specifically to the practice of taking lucrative high-level jobs in private industry with the help of their agencies where they were formerly employed and in industries that are regulated by those agencies (this is the usual image of *amakudari* in the public imagination). In actuality, many of the retiring bureaucrats find jobs in various types of government-owned or supported organizations. This practice probably came to be called *amakudari* because bureaucrats consider their jobs to be the most prestigious of all: the government agencies are "heaven," and all other employers inhabit lesser worlds below.

Most Japanese employers theoretically operate under a lifetime employment system: an employee works for the same company or organization until he or she reaches retirement age at about fifty-five or sixty. This is not the case with the bureaucracy. The nature of the bureaucratic system today dictates that almost every bureaucrat has to retire early, and retired bureaucrats must "descend from heaven" to work in the private sector because government pensions are too low to retire upon.

In order to understand the importance of *amakudari* in Japan's bureaucratic system, it is helpful to make a comparison with American government personnel practices. In the U.S. system, a number of the highest officials are appointed by the president and take office upon confirmation by the Senate. Theoretically, it makes no difference whether or not presidential appointees were previously government employees. In Japan, high officials, specifically those with the ranking of director-general, or bureau chief, and higher, are appointed by the appropriate minister of state upon approval from a Cabinet presided over by the prime minister. In actuality, this is only a formal procedure. The Cabinet meeting is practically a rubber stamp for nominees appointed by an agency's bureaucrats. It is unthinkable for non-bureaucrats, particularly private citizens, to become high officials. It is true that there have been exceptions, including, for example, the appointment of a novelist as head of the Agency for Cultural Affairs. However, this appointment was considered a fluke and attributed to the weakness of bureaucrats presiding at the Ministry of Education of the time. Other agencies would never have tolerated such deviation from the norm. Indeed, in the ranks of Japan's government personnel, bureaucrats dominate important posts. Private citizens, no matter how capable and experienced, rarely get an opportunity to serve as high officials.

One consequence of this invariable practice of filling top-level positions with elite bureaucrats is that these same bureaucrats must end up being driven from government agencies at a relatively early stage in their career. Japan's bureaucracy operates not on the basis of merit but on length of service; the most important criterion is what year a bureaucrat began serving at the agency. Among the bureaucratic elite, a later entrant can never surpass an earlier entrant in rank or salary. Only one of those who enter in a particular year can become administrative vice-minister, the highest post a bureaucrat can attain. The term of office for an administrative vice-minister is, as a rule, one year, which means that the person appointed must usually make room for another appointee by retiring at the age of fifty-five or fifty-six. The pyramid structure also forces many officials into retirement at a much earlier age than necessary because so few can make it to the top. By the time bureaucrats reach their mid-forties, they are gradually pressured to retire from government service, with the exception of those deemed candidate material for administrative vice-minister or director-general. An agency's personnel office transfers as many early retirees as possible into government-owned or supported organizations or into auxiliary organizations of the agencies themselves. If there is no room for retirees in those organizations, then personnel officers urge private sector industries and companies under their agency's jurisdiction to accept these early retirees. These companies cannot refuse to hire the retirees because bureaucracy will not take no for an answer.

Even for those bureaucrats who reach the highest positions in the bureaucracy, *amakudari* has now become necessary. This is a stark reversal of their privileged prewar work conditions. Until the end of World War II, bureaucrats enjoyed their status as "the Emperor's officials" receiving far better compensation than private-sector workers and retiring comfortably on generous pensions and allowances. The enforced democratization of Japan after World War II turned the tables on bureaucrats, who lost many of their special privileges. Today, University of Tokyo graduates who work for commercial banks, securities companies, and *shosha* (trading companies) are paid much higher salaries than those who become bureaucrats. In addition, the average life expectancy of the Japanese has increased dramatically since the war, from approximately fifty-one to eighty. Even an administrative vice-minister at the Ministry of Finance, which is perhaps the most prestigious position in the bureaucracy, cannot afford to live in Japan on a pension alone. He has to accept *amakudari* just like any other bureaucrat, working until reaching age seventy or beyond at a second career found for him by his agency's personnel section. In short, the Japanese bureaucracy functions with the premise that most bureaucrats will move on to an *amakudari* position. If *amakudari* positions were to become scarce, the next generation of Japanese would not be as interested in becoming bureaucrats. If a bureaucratic career loses its prestigious aura, the system will be endangered.

Thus all agencies try their hardest to secure the best *amakudari* prospects for their retirees. There are basically three ways to do so. One way is to win as large a budget as possible for one's own agency from the Ministry of Finance, in order to enlarge the government-owned organizations that fall under the agency's jurisdiction so that retirees may be sent to them. A second way is for the agency to ask industries under its jurisdiction to set up various foundations, that can serve as destinations for *amakudari*. The third and most valuable route is to promote the industries under agency jurisdiction. The Ministry of Finance backs the banking, securities, and insurance industries; MITI, manufacturing; the Ministry of Health and Welfare, the pharmaceutical industry; the Ministry of Construction, the construction industry; the Ministry of Agriculture, the food industry; and the Ministry of Transport, the transportation and tourism industries. Agencies will do whatever benefits their industries' interests, even if it comes to waging jurisdictional battles against other agencies. Agencies want to ensure that their respective industries owe them a favor so that *amakudari* prospects for their retirees are secure. As many bureaucrats put it, the relationship between the bureaucracy and industry is characterized by an inextricable interdependence.

However, many major industrialists in Japan have not been pleased with what they view as the bureaucracy's self-important attitude. While industrialists give credit to the bureaucracy for its role in Japan's economic development, particularly the postwar recovery, more and more of them would prefer that bureaucracy keep out of private sector activities. As the Japanese economy grew, a number of companies in industries such as banking, trading, automotive, consumer electronics, and semiconductors attained global-level reputations. They tend to believe that Japan has become an economic superpower largely due to the efforts of private enterprise, and not so much because of the efforts of the bureaucracy. As evidence of this sentiment, major companies nowadays are reluctant to accept retired bureaucrats as employees under *amakudari*. Even officials at the powerful Ministry of Finance have virtually no chance of securing an important executive position at such prestigious banks as Mitsubishi, Sumitomo, Dai-Ichi Kangyo, or the Industrial Bank of Japan. At the last minute, a former administrative vice-minister at MITI was turned down by a Mitsubishi chemical company, although he had been scheduled to be hired into the fast-track path that would have eventually led to the company's presidency. *Amakudari* prospects for MITI bureaucrats are becoming increasingly limited to electric power companies, steel manufacturers, and consumer electronics companies, all of which are under MITI's strong control. Moreover, the Japanese media are growing increasingly critical of *amakudari*.

While industry leaders are very respectful to incumbent bureaucrats, even to the relatively lowly section chiefs, the road is not necessarily smooth for all bureaucrats after retirement. To gain a good *amakudari* post, one must have at least become a bureau chief while in the bureaucracy. This is one reason why competition for promotion within the bureaucracy is intensifying.

Interdependence of Bureaucracy and Industry
Despite a growing resistance to the practice among some business leaders, *amakudari*, with its image of deities descending from heaven to work among ordinary people, continues to symbolize the mutually beneficial relationship between the bureaucracy and the Japanese

economy. Former bureaucrats, with their connections to their former agencies, can be a valuable link in coordinating between the government and industry.

Bureaucrats consider the protection and promotion of industries under their jurisdiction as their most important mission. They can make it extremely hard for new businesses to enter an industry through their power to grant licenses. Industry, on the other hand, maintains close ties to the bureaucrats and makes certain that government policy is in its interest. In return for the protection of the bureaucracy, industry accepts a number of bureaucrats for *amakudari* after they retire from government service. If a company in a particular industry opposes the way the bureaucracy does business or rejects retiring officials for *amakudari*, that company is bound to receive unfavorable treatment from the bureaucracy. The bureaucracy has enormous clout in general and controls a large portion of the national budget. Any company or financial organization that rebels against the bureaucracy, including global giants such as Toyota, NEC, Honda, Mitsubishi Heavy Industries, Nippon Life Insurance, and the Industrial Bank of Japan, does so at its peril.

Since companies know full well that they cannot out-maneuver the bureaucracy, they usually let the bureaucracy know what their wishes are before it finalizes its policies and seek a compromise in case of disagreement. It is interesting that bureaucrats are most likely to listen to those major companies founded in Tokyo. MITI, for instance, lends a sympathetic ear to the following companies in various industries: Nippon Steel (steel); Toshiba (consumer electric appliances); Mitsubishi Heavy Industries (machinery); and Tokyo Electric Power (electric power). Toyota and NEC, for example, are outside the inner circle of MITI because both had begun their business outside of Tokyo.

The Ministry of Finance plays favorites in a similar fashion: it tends to listen more to banks that have its headquarters in Tokyo such as Mitsubishi Bank and Fuji Bank than to others. For example, because Sumitomo Bank's headquarters are located in Osaka, it has been considered an "outsider." An influential director-general at MITI attests: "We at MITI have confidence in those companies that have been in Tokyo for a long time, such as the Mitsubishi and Mitsui groups. Not only do we frequently meet with people from those companies, but those companies have Japan's national interest in mind, and operate accordingly. We can talk policy in an open manner with those companies."

Major companies obey the bureaucracy and accept *amakudari* officials because staying on good terms is in their own interest. On the other hand, bureaucrats can give orders to presidents of major companies because the bureaucracy wields such powerful influence through its authority to license and to enforce regulations. Bureaucrats would not dream of giving up their power to regulate industry, and they strongly resist attempts to deregulate Japan's economy or reassess licensing procedures. An official at the Ministry of Transport, which probably has more licensing power than any other agency, states: "The administration of transportation is very important for the safety of the general public. While deregulation is a fine concept, excessive deregulation would threaten public safety, and public criticism would be directed at the Ministry of Transport." However, this opinion can be viewed in part as an attempt to protect the ministry's turf. The Ministry of Transport most certainly wants to retain its regulatory power over such industries as airlines, shipping, and railways, and to ensure these companies continue to create *amakudari* positions.

Ironically, MITI's status within the Japanese government is considered to have declined in recent years; the industries that have been under MITI's nurture and care have grown so strong that they no longer require MITI's help. Moreover, MITI has been voluntarily loosening its regulation of them, which has been a factor in its declining influence over them. Other government agencies are doing their best to delay deregulation, largely with the intent of avoiding MITI's fate. Even if a powerful administration expended all of its political capital in an attempt to bring about deregulation, it would probably fail to overcome the all-out resistance that would be put forth by bureaucrats and industry. The alliance of bureaucracy and industry dies hard.

As mentioned earlier, bureaucrats, industries and *zoku* politicians (legislators with special interest in, and ties to, political causes closely associated with the ministries) have forged a strong alliance that is often called the Iron Triangle. The bureaucracy has formed the solid base of this triangle through its ability to secure increases in budget allocations for itself, and by distributing the money to industries to secure the prospects for *amakudari* of its retiring officials. Although the triangle has thrived under the thirty-eight years of LDP rule, its resilient structure has led to a number of serious problems. An obvious problem is that the structure of the bureaucracy is still designed to promote and protect industry even though Japan is now an economic giant and no longer needs a protected economy. One result is that Japan has incurred a huge trade surplus that has been the focus of criticism from a number of countries. While public administration is designed to enhance inter-industry competitiveness, the gates leading to Japanese markets have been relatively difficult for foreign companies to open. Distribution of foreign goods in Japan is particularly difficult. It is no wonder that foreign nations complain about the closed nature of Japanese markets.

There are also domestic consequences created by the Iron Triangle. As the components of the triangle reached a state of equilibrium, budget allocation by the government became rigid. A budget should respond to changes in economic circumstances, but case-by-case flexibility has been impossible because of the triangle structure. As the licensing powers of the bureaucracy increased, inefficient sectors of the economy were preserved. This is one reason for Japan's extremely high consumer prices. According to a recent issue of the *Nippon Keizai Shimbun*, a major daily economic newspaper, consumer goods in New York and Tokyo had the following price differences:

Item	New York	Tokyo
Butter (450 g / 1 lb)	$1.90	$7.16
Milk (3.79 l / 1 gal)	$2.19	$8.64
Sirloin steak (450 g / 1 lb)	$4.20	$62.79
Toilet paper (6 rolls)	$1.99	$2.99
Video rental (48 hours)	$2.00	$2.90

According to one bureaucrat interviewed, many in the bureaucracy have complained about Japan's ridiculously high consumer prices: "The government has not done anything for the consumer. It is time for us to shift our emphasis from producer-oriented to consumer-oriented public administration." A number of young, promising bureaucrats who have grown tired of an "antiquated system incapable of changing with the times" have abandoned the bureaucracy to start over in the private sector.

Can the System Change?

The LDP's one-party rule came to an end at a time when the bureaucracy was under fire from all sides. The Hosokawa and Hata administrations were intent on deregulation and structural reform of the bureaucracy. The LDP subsequently came back to power by forming a coalition with the Social Democratic Party of Japan, its former arch-rival; however, the trend towards deregulation and bureaucratic reform has not altered.The new direction in politics was forced upon the leadership by city dwellers whose very efforts had made Japan's spectacular economic growth possible. Fed up with a political and economic system that did not adequately reward them for their work, they started to demand a new system that served the interests of the ordinary citizen and consumer rather than the producer. Business leaders, as well, called for reform of Japan's political and economic system. They proclaimed: "Stop artificially preserving inefficient business sectors. Let the market system take care of itself and bring prices down."

Why have these business leaders, once an integral part of the Iron Triangle, begun speaking out like this? One reason is that Japanese companies that have become global giants are beginning to feel that government intervention is a nuisance. Business leaders believe that Japan's regulations, especially concerning licensing, have become unacceptable worldwide. They have come to believe that increasing market share abroad while maintaining Japan's protective system is not only hypocritical, but would cause trade disputes to worsen. In addition, industrialists want to make room for new businesses in domestic markets as an attempt to end the current recession in Japan.

In any event, many factions are calling for deregulation. But, is there any hope for reforming Japan's antiquated bureaucracy?

Prospects for reform are slim, but not hopeless. A major barrier to reform is the difficulty of coming to an agreed-upon solution. While it is true that politicians, major industrialists, the urban salaried workers who are known as "company warriors," and some bureaucrats are demanding deregulation, they do not agree on what specific measures to take. For example, business leaders who are vocal proponents of deregulation do not approve of measures that they think would hurt their companies. Few factions want total deregulation.

An incident at MITI a few years ago is a telling example of the difference between deregulation in rhetoric and in practice. A head of the Petroleum Department at the Agency of Natural Resources and Energy sought to ease regulations on service stations and introduce more competition into the gasoline business. High officials at MITI were hardly enthusiastic about this official's project; they considered such deregulation unnecessary. The department head did not give up, however, and was successful in convincing MITI officials of the necessity for deregulation. However, the LDP legislators who are identified with the petroleum business opposed deregulation, and the petroleum-related businesses that feared deregulation undertook a preposterous campaign to obstruct the project by printing a leaflet featuring a photograph of the official and a fabricated list of his "wrongdoings." Thousands of these leaflets were distributed throughout Kasumigaseki. Other attempts were undertaken to stop this department head, but he refused to give up and finally succeeded in deregulating gasoline stations. A high transport official commented on the episode: "Compared with industries supervised by the Ministry of Transport, MITI's industries resemble the boy scouts. If the Ministry of Transport got really serious about deregulation, it would receive threats from the yakuza (gangsters). Officials would have reason to fear for their lives."

Any attempt at deregulation thus faces fierce opposition from those who feel their interests are at risk. In addition, bureaucrats who take the initiative on behalf of deregulation cannot expect to be rewarded by the system. The official in the above story did not advance his career by taking charge of the issue.

A division chief at the Ministry of Agriculture, Forestry, and Fisheries provides further explanation on why the bureaucracy cannot change itself, reduce licenses, or cut a bloated budget: "Let's suppose that my division streamlined itself and asked for less money than last year. The money saved would just be allocated to another section, it would not go back to the taxpayers. In other words, even if one division tries to save money, the ministry as a whole does not change. The ministry would not even dream of asking for less money than it did in the past year because issuing licenses and getting as large a portion of the national budget as possible is evidence to the public that the ministry is doing a lot of work. It follows that if I reduce the number of licenses and asked for less money for my division, my subordinates might be pleased because I cut their workload. But in the ministry, I would get a reputation as a slacker. That is the way of the bureaucracy."

As we have seen, the Japanese bureaucracy is not structured in a way that it can reform itself. Only two possible ways to carry out reform seem available: one is by *gaiatsu* ("foreign pressure"), the other is through strong political leadership. However, since August 1993, politicians have been even weaker than they had been under the previous decades of LDP domination. Political leadership cannot influence a strong bureaucracy when it is fragmented, as evidenced by the fact that three different coalitions held power in one year. While the bureaucracy has become stronger, political coalitions have become weaker than ever.

Because of Japan's weak political leadership, movement for deregulation may slow down a little, at least temporarily. But the cause will not die. There inevitably will be strong opposition to deregulation from all sides of the Iron Triangle, but this must be overcome in the quest for reform. Even bureaucrats who usually fight one another over territory and influence have come to recognize a need for reform. They may resist reform at their own agencies, but few seem to actually believe that the bureaucracy as a whole is wonderful the way it is, or that it does not need to change. A number of young bureaucrats in their twenties and thirties are frustrated with the status quo. Many confidently declare: "When we become high officials, we will enact reform!"

The problem is that the bureaucracy as whole does not necessarily move in the same direction as its individual members; that is the main barrier to reforming the bureaucratic structure. Even if reform-minded bureaucrats constituted a majority in an agency, reform would not be much easier. It would still take a great deal of energy and creativity to make a break from stagnant organization.

Of course, reform must be demanded by the Japanese people. If they do nothing about the current state of the bureaucracy, Japan will continue to be a giant exporter, "company warriors" will be less motivated, and the global community will isolate the nation for being selfish and closed. To prevent such an outcome, Japan needs to invite foreign criticism. How Japanese politics and bureaucracy will respond to criticism from the outside remains to be seen, but I hope that Western readers will keep a sympathetic eye on Japan's struggle to change.

2

THE BUREAUCRACY AND TRADE CONFLICT

Blundering through U.S.–Japan Relations

A growing desire to reassess U.S.–Japan relations is emerging from such powerful government agencies as the Ministry of Foreign Affairs, MITI, and the Ministry of Finance. While these ministry bureaucrats were formerly interested only in maintaining Japan's friendly ties to the United States, this is no longer the case. The most important reason behind their change of attitude is the collapse of communism in the Soviet Union and Eastern Europe, resulting in the end of the Cold War. According to a high-ranking foreign affairs official: "Japan has prospered largely due to the U.S.–Japan Security Treaty and the U.S. 'nuclear umbrella.' We must always be grateful to the United States for this. But today, relations between the two nations need adjustment because of the collapse of the Soviet Union. Japan should not continue to depend unilaterally on the U.S. but should take responsibility as an equal partner. We ought to talk straight with the U.S."

A high official at MITI echoes this sentiment: "U.S. foreign policy always reflects America's self-interest, and no one else's. Now that

Japan has the second largest GNP in the world, Japan and the United States sometimes may not see eye to eye. Now that the U.S. has formed a regional economic bloc called the North American Free Trade Agreement (NAFTA), Japan may have to respond in kind by forming a similar economic bloc in Asia."

Japanese bureaucrats harbor a deeply-rooted distrust of U.S. motives. They seem to think that the Americans would do anything to further their self-interest, even in violation of the General Agreement on Tariffs and Trade (GATT). In particular, the revival of the so-called "Super 301" trade law provision by the Clinton administration outraged Japanese bureaucrats, who viewed it as an American attempt to blame Japan for its own problems. Since 1992 MITI has issued an Annual Report on Unfair Trade Policy with the aim of proving the unfairness of American trade practices in light of GATT rules.

Throughout its thirty-eight years in power, the LDP kept in check the Japanese bureaucracy's distrust of the U.S., and worked to maintain good U.S.–Japan relations. The LDP knew how to deal effectively with the Americans, and it kept the bureaucracy under control. However, now that the LDP's political era has come to an end, politicians have far less control over bureaucracy. On February 11, 1994, Prime Minister Hosokawa and President Clinton failed to reach agreement on trade issues. The primary reason for the failure on the Japanese side was the inability of the Hosokawa administration to gain an upper hand over the bureaucracy. Says a Ministry of Foreign Affairs official who took part in the trade negotiations: "Quite a few bureaucrats, not just foreign affairs officials, but also those from other agencies such as the Ministry of Finance and MITI, have improved their debating skills while studying abroad and on overseas assignments. At the negotiation table, bureaucrats from both countries waged a war of words, but the Americans seemed intimidated and surprised by their Japanese counterparts because the Japanese proved more eloquent and logical than the Americans had anticipated."

Usually, Japanese bureaucrats who serve as negotiators in such discussions will lose heart and look dejected over a failure to reach agreement. After the talks failed between Hosokawa and Clinton, however, the bureaucrats emanated an aura of victory. Despite their small victory and their air of confidence, however, the manner in which Japanese bureaucrats negotiate with foreign countries indicates a number of serious problems within the bureaucracy. When it comes to economic issues, for example, foreign affairs officials are powerless in the Japanese bureaucracy. During the recent U.S.–Japan trade negotiations, the Ministry of Finance addressed macroeconomics and insurance issues, while MITI was in charge of the automobile issue. The Ministry of Foreign Affairs had no place of authority. Bureaucrats at the other agencies openly deride the Ministry of Foreign Affairs, saying that it has no purpose other than to take care of diplomatic protocol.

Another indicator of internal problems at Kasumigaseki is that powerful agencies such as the Ministry of Finance and MITI have formed overseas networks completely separate from the Ministry of Foreign Affairs. For example, the Ministry of Finance has stationed approximately twenty bureaucrats in the U.S. at such government offices as the Japanese Embassy in Washington, D.C., the Japanese Consulate-General in New York, the World Bank, and the U.S. offices of the Export-Import Bank of Japan. MITI has stationed even more people in the U.S. than the Ministry of Finance. Both these agencies conduct intelligence activities that are totally separate from those of the Ministry of Foreign Affairs.

Communications among Japan's various government agencies are extremely rare: no agency shares important information with the others. Interministry battles for influence and power thus extend far beyond Japan's borders. In an extreme case, the Ministry of Finance purposely withheld from the Ministry of Foreign Affairs the secret dispatch of a mission abroad to negotiate global currency issues. Japan's foreign economic policy evidently lacks a united front. To rectify this situation, the Cabinet Secretariat set up the Councillor's Office on External Affairs; however, these efforts have been to no avail. One foreign affairs official, fed up with the lack of unity among agencies, expressed the feeling that, under these circumstances, it is impossible for Japanese bureaucrats to deal comprehensively with the U.S. on either the political or economic front. The disunity may very well be the Achilles' heel of the Japanese bureaucracy.

MITI in the Middle

Several years ago during a discussion I was having with MITI bureaucrats, one official suddenly burst out: "Japanese companies are market-share oriented and selfish. They export like crazy and cause problems with the U.S., Europe, everywhere. We did not become MITI officials to clean up their messes!"

MITI officials hold various opinions on what to do about recurring trade friction. Quite a few believe that from now on MITI should take on the task of settling trade disputes rather than promoting Japanese industry, since Japanese companies now have a secure foundation. However, as one may guess from the above outburst, MITI is very frustrated in deciding what its role in government should be in the future. As Japanese companies have grown competitive in global markets with the help of MITI, at the same time they have started to act contrary to MITI's recommendations. MITI has asked companies not to engage in offensive export practices that would disrupt foreign markets, but few companies have complied with their suggestions.

At one time, few companies dissented from MITI's directives. When the Japanese economy was recovering from the devastation of World War II, MITI controlled precious foreign currency reserves and limited the introduction of foreign investment and technology. A company that disobeyed MITI did so knowing fully that MITI would retaliate. In the late 1960s, however, MITI began to deregulate the administration of trade and capital, a measure that became necessary after Japan joined the Organization for Economic Cooperation and Development (OECD) in 1964, thereby entering the ranks of developed countries. After deregulation, MITI found it difficult to keep companies on as tight a leash as it had before; it had abandoned an effective means of control. As a result of its great success in promoting Japanese industry, MITI has rendered itself less powerful. A MITI official lamented, "Japanese companies have grown thanks to MITI's policy, but they are ungrateful."

Contributing to MITI's recent frustrations is the fact that while it has deregulated the industries under its supervision to a considerable degree, other agencies have not cooperated in achieving their share of deregulation. On the contrary, other agencies have acted to further protect their industries: the Ministry of Finance continues to protect the finance, insurance, and securities industries; the Ministry of Agriculture, Forestry, and Fisheries, agricultural products such as rice; and the Ministry of Construction, public works projects. If those agencies had followed MITI's example and deregulated the industries under their jurisdictions, their influence over them would have decreased and finding positions for *amakudari* would have become difficult. Therefore, those agencies are in all likelihood glad to not have fallen into MITI's present predicament.

Many of Japan's government agencies actually blame MITI for the mounting pressure from foreign countries to open Japanese markets. Products under MITI supervision, such as automobiles, consumer electric appliances, and semiconductors, have been a primary focus of international trade disputes, and the other agencies believe that the fault lies with MITI for having let the industries loose in the first place. Because of this belief, these other agencies are unreceptive to MITI's requests for further market opening and deregulation, claiming: "MITI will have the authority to tell us what to do when it succeeds in stemming the excessive export of Japan's industrial products." MITI has difficulty finding an effective response to such an accusation.

However, MITI has been on the right track as far as deregulation is concerned. Other agencies, albeit gradually and in response to foreign pressure, are beginning to deregulate their industries. "Other agencies would not listen to MITI's requests," a top MITI official maintains. "To make them listen, foreign demands to open Japanese markets are welcome, because they are particularly effective. Unfortunately, Japan lacks the ability to deregulate on its own. It would be great if politics underwent a drastic change, but I wouldn't bet on it happening anytime soon."

MITI faces a dilemma: while it has been a pioneer in the Japanese government through its efforts to deregulate, its efforts have been viewed by the other agencies as indirectly responsible for the resulting trade disputes. While younger MITI officials are arguing that MITI should take on the role of a "think tank" for the bureaucracy, the other agencies are not likely to heed their advice. MITI's dilemma, then, is simultaneously the dilemma of the Japanese nation.

A Foreign Policy Debacle

The U.S.–Japan Comprehensive Economic Talks that began in September 1993 were suspended in February 1994 with President Clinton and Prime Minister Hosokawa failing to reach agreement on the issues discussed. The focus of these talks had not been macroeconomic policy but three specific issues: government procurement, insurance, and automobiles and automobile parts. The Americans firmly demanded that Japan institute "objective standards" in these three areas to "measure the degree of openness of the Japanese markets," and that these standards should be measured numerically. However, the Japanese adamantly opposed the institution of numerical targets. They argued that numerical targets are tantamount to "managed trade," as well as counterproductive to the deregulation efforts that were being promoted by the Hosokawa administration. The two sides argued back and forth over whether the "objective standards" were numerical targets and whether Japan would be forced to practice managed trade, leading one negotiator to criticize the talks as a "theological debate." The issues ultimately could not be resolved before the meeting between the two countries' leaders.

Many of the negotiators on the Japanese side appeared smug about the failure of the talks; they considered themselves victorious in rejecting the nonsensical American demands. But a number of Japanese government insiders were critical of the negotiators for damaging friendly U.S.–Japan relations by their insistence on the "theological debate." Interestingly, a number of influential politicians from all parties said that the talks failed because bureaucrats were in charge of the negotiations.

Each area of the negotiations was addressed by a different agency: the Ministry of Foreign Affairs handled government procurement; the Ministry of Finance, insurance; and MITI, automobiles and automobile parts. Government procurement was an issue affecting the jurisdictions of several agencies responsible for the purchase of foreign goods and services. For this reason, the Ministry of Health and Welfare, which is directly involved in the purchase of medical equipment; the Ministry of Posts and Telecommunications, which oversees the Nippon Telegraph and Telephone Corporation (NTT); the Ministry of Education, and the Science and Technology Agency all joined the discussions. Since the Ministry of Foreign Affairs lacked the clout to lead these agencies in the negotiations, MITI took the role of coordinator. MITI officials then asked the Ministry of Health and Welfare and the Ministry of Posts and Telecommunications to give some concessions in government procurement to ensure a secure negotiating position with the Americans.

However, the Japanese and American negotiators failed to reach an agreement on government procurement, which had seemed at first to be the most promising of the three areas. A Japanese negotiator commented: "the Americans' top priority was automobiles and automobile parts. The failure of the talks in this area made compromises in government procurement absolutely worthless." Why then did MITI ask the other agencies to compromise on government procurement when MITI did not give the Americans an inch on automobiles and automobile parts? A MITI bureaucrat who played a central role in the talks stated: "I think the American government misunderstood Japan. Japanese consumers welcome U.S. pressure to open Japanese markets for American agricultural products such as beef and oranges because they like those products. But automobiles are another matter. The Japanese people have a negative image of American automobiles. We cannot make the Japanese public purchase what it considers to be inferior products."

This view is shared by many MITI officials, but there are other reasons why MITI did not give concessions to the Americans on automobiles and automobile parts. The primary reason is that the Japanese auto industry had been in a recession. If the auto industry were booming, MITI might have gotten some concessions from it, but the reality was otherwise. The auto industry, in fact, had firmly requested that MITI not compromise with the Americans. Another reason is a general distrust of the Americans stemming from bitterness over the U.S.–Japan agreement on semiconductors in 1986 and the Global Partnership "Action Plan" on automobiles of January 1992 when President Bush visited Japan. In these agreements, it was MITI's intent to include numerical figures only as a "guideline for the private sector." The Americans, however, viewed those figures to be literal numerical goals, and demanded that Japan attain them. In short, MITI officials feel that whatever numerical goals are discussed may be later seized on by the Americans as target shortfalls and that they should not even be discussing numbers with the Americans in the first place. In fact, MITI bureaucrats had not given up all hope for reaching an agreement on automobiles and automobile parts. In response to American demands, they had repeatedly asked the Japanese auto industry to increase purchases of foreign parts and persuaded the Ministry of Transport to give concessions on the licensing and admitting of foreign automobiles.

The Ministry of Transport is responsible for administering all aspects of transportation in Japan. A large agency with personnel numbering approximately 38,000, almost four times MITI's 10,500, its responsibilities include land, sea, and air transportation; tourism; the Maritime Safety Agency; and the Meteorological Agency. Despite its size, the Ministry of Transport has largely been known as a "licensing agency" or an "on-site agency" and has historically not been as powerful an economic agency as MITI. This is because of the domination of the ministry by transport officials with technical backgrounds, that is, people who were successful candidates for the Level I Entrance Examination after majoring in the natural sciences or engineering. While those who studied law or economics hold important posts such as administrative vice-minister or director-general of the secretariat, they cannot interfere with the administration of individual technical fields. For example, the ministry's Road Transport Bureau has an Engineering and Safety Department that is staffed almost entirely by officials with technical or engineering backgrounds. It is a veritable "Kingdom of Technology Officials." This department supervises Japan's infamous perfectionist automobile inspection system. It is said that in the U.S. eleven states do not even require regular inspection of automobiles by law; however, in Japan, the national government requires an automobile inspection in every prefecture. In fact, a tune-up is required before the regular inspection.

Japanese drivers have been for some time fed up with these strict automobile regulations, demanding longer intervals between regular inspections (because of the greater reliability of automobiles) and advocating the abolition of the requisite pre-inspection tune-up. However, the ministry's Engineering and Safety Department consistently ignores the public's demands and lobbies key Diet members to maintain the status quo. Automobile inspection and tune-up businesses employ some 380,000 workers, and the division's technology officials are doing their best to protect these people's interests. Although they have not spoken out, transport bureaucrats with backgrounds in law or economics oppose these policies, but cannot outmaneuver the united front of the technology officials and their effective campaign to lobby influential politicians. This is just one illustration of divisiveness in the Japanese bureaucracy, not just between the ministries but within a single ministry. As a popular bureaucratic saying goes: "There are bureaus and sections, but no ministry." Individual bureaus and sections form "sovereign kingdoms" by allying themselves with industries and politicians and looking after their own self-interests.

Yet, this entrenched Engineering and Safety Department eventually began to give substantial concessions to the Americans on automobile inspections and importing procedures. Apparently, the reason behind these concessions is that *gaiatsu* ("foreign pressure") from the U.S. helped the transport bureaucrats to persuade its technology officials to give in to some of the American's demands.

On March 11, 1994, a month after the failure of the U.S.–Japan Talks, the Japanese government notified the U.S. government that it would accept the "Motorola mobile phone agreement." Previously, on February 15, U.S. Trade Representative Mickey Kantor had announced that the Japanese mobile communications market, which includes car and cellular phones, had not met the level of openness agreed to by the two countries in 1989 and that the U.S. would begin to impose sanctions on Japan. The Japanese government was extremely concerned that the already troubled relations between the two countries would get worse. To the rescue came Ozawa Ichiro, former secretary-general of the ruling LDP, co-founder of the Japan Renewal Party, and probably the most powerful politician in Japan, to offer behind-the-scenes support of the Hosokawa administration. In urging the government to accept the U.S. demands on this particular issue, Ozawa seemed to believe that further deterioration of U.S.–Japan relations would jeopardize the Hosokawa administration's popularity on the domestic front. Ozawa directly asked the Ministry of Posts and Telecommunications to settle the matter quickly by giving concessions to the U.S.

The Ministry of Posts and Telecommunications is responsible for administering electronic communications and broadcasting, the Postal Service, life insurance affiliated with the Postal Service, and the postal savings system. The last named is a financial institution that holds the largest deposits of savings by individuals in the world. The ministry is becoming increasingly prominent in the government as the fields of electronic communications and broadcasting, which it administers, become more and more crucial to an information-oriented modern society. Furthermore, the ministry has a reputation for wielding great political influence. Upon the inauguration of the Hosokawa administration following the defeat of the LDP in August 1993, the ministry strengthened its ties with Ozawa Ichiro, and it soon came to be known as "Ozawa's Ministry." The ministry's strategy within the bureaucracy has been to counter powerful agencies such as MITI and the Ministry of Finance by winning powerful politicians over to its side. Therefore, it could not refuse the request from Ozawa, its most important patron and the mastermind of the Hosokawa administration'spolitical agenda.

Some in the ministry argued that to yield on the Motorola issue would be to sell out Japan's sovereign control of its telecommunications industry for the sake of a single American company. But such voices were soon suppressed, and the ministry agreed to give the Americans exactly what they wanted. The ministry promised, in the "Motorola mobile phone agreement," that Japan Mobile Communications (abbreviated IDO in Japanese), a private company, would set up 159 mobile telephone bases for Motorola and that the Japanese government would support this move through "all available measures."

Thus, while the Japanese government had fiercely opposed numerical targets in the U.S.–Japan Comprehensive Economic Talks, it had approved them for a company called Motorola. Why? There may be reasons other than Ozawa's influence. First of all, the Ministry of Posts and Telecommunications has a certain degree of flexibility that the Ministry of Finance and MITI do not have. The telecommunications officials seem to be realists rather than idealists, and do not appear to mind making changes in important policy, unlike the officials of other agencies. If MITI had been in charge of the Motorola issue, for example, concessions would never have been made. Proud bureaucrats at the Ministry of Finance, MITI and Ministry of Home Affairs usually reject any idea that goes against their fundamental policy, no matter which powerful politician makes the request.

Another possible reason for this capitulation on the Motorola issue is that the Ministry of Finance, MITI, and the Ministry of Foreign Affairs, having taken the blame for the failure of the Comprehensive Economic Talks, attempted to make up for this by having the Ministry of Posts and Telecommunications yield to the Americans. For compelling evidence, consider that some of the largest IDO shareholders include Tokyo Electric Power and automakers such as Toyota and Nissan, all of which are industries supervised by MITI. It is probable that MITI asked those corporations to cooperate to prevent the decline in U.S.–Japan relations. The Ministry of Finance and Ministry of Foreign Affairs also supported the Ministry of Posts and Telecommunications on this issue.

When the Japanese government declared its refusal to accept "numerical targets," it should have consistently applied that policy on the telecommunications issue. The Ministry of Finance, MITI, and the Ministry of Foreign Affairs all accepted the Ministry of Posts and Telecommunications' change in government policy without criticism: since they were not directly in charge of the issue, they did not feel accountable. As one can see from these examples, Japanese bureaucracy has no comprehensive strategy to deal with international trade issues. With such a narrow vision, the bureaucracy can only protect its self-interest and must rely on *gaiatsu* to change policy.

3

THE MAKING OF THE ELITE

On the Winning Track

Japanese bureaucrats enjoy a high status in society. Theoretically, whether or not an individual becomes a bureaucrat depends entirely on his or her ability. When the national civil service exams are being scored, whether one's father is a powerful politician or a fabulously wealthy industrialist makes no difference. On the contrary, even if one comes from a poor family, passing the Level I Entrance Examination for the National Civil Service or the Diplomatic Service Examination would make him or her a worthy member of the establishment.

The Level I Entrance Examination for the National Civil Service ranks alongside the National Bar Exam as one of the two most competitive examinations even in an increasingly competitive Japan. In 1993, of the 35,887 candidates who took the Level I Entrance Examination, only 1,863 passed, evidencing a daunting success rate of one out of nineteen. But passing this exam does not necessarily mean that one will get a position in a government agency. Only a total of 1,012 positions, or one out of approximately 35.5, were available that year in all the agencies concerned. What makes the competition even tougher is that only those who have majored in law or economics can realistically hope to move up in the bureaucracy to become administrative vice-ministers or director-generals. Also consider that about one-half of all successful law or economics majors who actually land government jobs are graduates of a single university: the University of Tokyo, appropriately nicknamed the "Preparatory Academy for Bureaucrats." Consequently, young people who want to pursue careers in the bureaucracy seek admission to the law department or economics department of this university.

The entrance exams for the University of Tokyo are the most difficult and competitive of the 514 four-year higher education institutions of Japan; even for the exceptionally bright student, it is extremely difficult to be admitted without preparing for these exams for years, and it has become increasingly essential to be enrolled at high schools whose graduates have been admitted to University of Tokyo at relatively high rates. Practically speaking, these high schools have become cram schools for admission to the University of Tokyo; they admit bright students from all over Japan and rigorously teach them the necessary skills for passing the entrance exams. Interestingly, virtually all of these are private schools. Of approximately 5,500 public high schools in Japan, only twenty or so schools have produced more than ten successful candidates for the University of Tokyo each year.

This vicious pattern actually begins to unfold even before high school; students must first seek admission to middle schools that have been successful in feeding their graduates into those rigorous high schools. This means that preparation to enter desirable middle schools must begin at the elementary school level. It is common for parents to hire private tutors to teach their children the necessary skills for gaining admission to the elementary, middle, and high schools that constitute the path to the University of Tokyo. Planning may even dictate the choice of a pre-school. Preparing children for admission to the University of Tokyo from such a young age is extremely expensive. For example, some parents living outside main urban areas believe that it is necessary to prepare their children for the middle school entrance exams by sending them to elementary schools in Tokyo or Osaka. Maintenance per child can cost tens of thousands of dollars a year.

Nowadays it is rare for children of rural families or modest means to graduate from a local high school and still gain admittance to the University of Tokyo. It is no coincidence that most of the successful candidates come from financially well-off families in major cities or suburbs. According to the *Asahi Shimbun Weekly AERA,* in 1989 the average household income of the families of those who were admitted to the University of Tokyo Law Department was ¥10,850,000 or approximately $78,600 at that time. Compare this figure to the national average Japanese household income of ¥5,950,000. Such statistics show that the parents of law students at the University of Tokyo are likely to be twice as wealthy as the average Japanese family. Moreover, fathers of successful candidates are well-educated: 70 percent have at least a bachelor's degree; some have postgraduate degrees; 10 percent are University of Tokyo alumni.

As stated earlier, becoming a bureaucrat depends in theory entirely on the individual candidate's ability. While the selection system of the bureaucracy is extremely fair in the sense that the scoring of the bureaucratic entrance exams is not influenced by such factors as a family's financial influence or social status, it is undeniable that these days most elite bureaucrats are children of wealthy, well-educated parents.

The Myth of the University of Tokyo

"Todai," the Japanese nickname for the University of Tokyo, is to would-be bureaucrats what a prestigious music school is to aspiring musicians. It was in 1878 that graduates of the then-new University of Tokyo first became bureaucrats, and for more than a century Todai alumni have dominated important government posts.

Nowadays, an increasing number of bureaucrats are alumni of other national institutions, such as the University of Kyoto and Hitotsubashi University, as well as of private universities such as Waseda and Keio Universities. Nevertheless, a student who attends Todai is more likely than a student of equal ability from another university to pass the Level I Entrance Examination for the National Civil Service and succeed in becoming a bureaucrat. Why? Consider the following factors.

First, the curriculum at the University of Tokyo is by tradition geared toward training potential bureaucrats. If a student attends classes regularly and understands the material taught, it is believed that the student requires no special preparation for the Level I Entrance Examination. Second, unlike other universities, Todai is attended by many students who aspire to be bureaucrats and there is a campus atmosphere that compels one to study hard for the goal of passing the exam. Third, many Todai alumni have become bureaucrats. Students can talk to them and ask for detailed tips on how to prepare for the exam.

However, the most important reason for the predominance of Todai graduates in the bureaucracy is their reputation. All the agencies that hire Todai graduates see them as reliable and bright. A Ministry of Finance planning officer who used to be in charge of recruitment explains: "A look at their university academic records reveals whether the students are bureaucrat material, even before they take the exam—provided that they are Todai students. Many Todai graduates become bureaucrats each year, and we in bureaucracy know what those standards mean. We know much less about students who were educated at other universities. Consequently, few non-Todai students become bureaucrats. Even if their academic records are good, we cannot evaluate them by Todai standards."

Powerful agencies such as the Ministry of Finance and MITI in fact hire bright Todai Law Department students regardless of other factors. These alumni have a privileged status in bureaucracy. Nevertheless, it would not be completely accurate to conclude that Todai-educated bureaucrats discriminate against bureaucrats who graduated from other universities. A MITI official who is a Todai graduate stated: "There is no faction of Todai alumni in the bureaucracy. There is no reason to have one because 90 percent of high officials in the Ministry of Finance and MITI are from the University of Tokyo. Todai graduates compete with one another for promotion, and they don't become allies just because they went to the same university. In contrast, bureaucrats from other universities such as Waseda and Keio are much more tightly united. But they cannot gain important posts through forming factions because there simply are not enough of them."

To sum it up, bright and talented youth aspiring to be high-ranking government officials enter the University of Tokyo, pass the Level I Entrance Examination with relative ease and become bureaucrats. These bureaucrats would likely counter criticism of the system with, "If you think Todai graduates monopolize the bureaucracy, then you should go to the University of Tokyo if you want to become a bureaucrat." Although the media criticize attitudes that serve to perpetuate the "omnipotent Todai" myth, as long as the University of Tokyo rules, the old habits will die hard.

An Insatiable Appetite for Top Graduates

On February 27, 1992, Prime Minister Miyazawa Kiichi called for government agencies to gradually quit the practice of hiring Todai graduates in undue proportions, and adhere to a recruitment policy emphasizing diversity. At a Cabinet meeting on the following day, Chief Cabinet Secretary Kato Koichi proposed that the proportion of Todai graduates in higher positions be reduced by 50 percent over the next five years. Cabinet members were asked to cooperate in the achievement of this goal.

Among the 508 successful candidates of the 1991 Level I Entrance Examination in the fields of public administration, law, and economics, 257, or nearly one-half, had been University of Tokyo graduates. Of the 310 successful candidates who were hired by all agencies, 182, or 59 percent, had been from the University of Tokyo. Furthermore, in each of the following nine agencies over 70 percent of the new recruits had been University of Tokyo graduates: MITI, Finance, Transport, Labor, Construction, Home Affairs, the National Police, Economic Planning and Agriculture, Forestry, and Fisheries. And three of these agencies, Finance, Home Affairs, and the National Police had obtained nearly 90 percent of their recruits from the University of Tokyo.

Were Prime Minister Miyazawa's guidelines adhered to at all? In 1992, the overall percentage of new recruits who were Todai graduates dropped by an insignificant 0.9 percent. In fact, six agencies, including Posts and Telecommunications, Environment, and Defense, seemed to have altogether ignored the Prime Minister's guidelines and increased the percentage of Todai graduates among their recruits. Chief Cabinet Secretary Kato summoned two high officials from the Ministry of Posts and Telecommunications to inquire why that agency acted contrary to the new guideline. The officials admitted that their ministry had hired more Todai students than allowed by the quota, and then explained that they had attempted to comply with the Cabinet resolution by accepting some ten students from other schools, but that most of them had ended up being taken by other agencies. The Ministry of Posts and Telecommunications officials, however, were not telling the whole story. What they did not admit was that the ministry had actually been very pleased to recruit as many University of Tokyo graduates as possible. In Kasumigaseki, a ministry's influence is unofficially measured by the number of University of Tokyo graduates hired. All agencies pursue and capture, with startling determination, as many University of Tokyo graduates as possible.

Questionable Hiring Rituals

As soon as the Japanese school year begins in April, officials in charge of recruitment from each ministry visit the University of Tokyo Law Department. These officials make the rounds of legal seminars that have a history of producing large numbers of bureaucrats, and, by July, each agency compiles a secret list of students who would make the most desirable recruits. This activity, though not legally binding, is in violation of college graduate hiring agreements which state that prospective employers should refrain from deciding which students to hire until a later date. But government agencies will do almost anything to recruit University of Tokyo students, even if it means breaking the rules, for their primary competitors are other agencies and not the private sector.

To relate a revealing incident: on the evening of an exceedingly hot day Saturday, August 4, 1990, recruitment officials of the Finance Minister's Secretariat contacted students from the ministry's secret list. This date was significant in Kasumigaseki, for the results of the Level I Entrance Examination were announced on July 23, and the second stage of the exams, the oral interviews, was to begin on August 7. During the early afternoon of August 4, other agencies had started to contact students on their respective secret lists, and pressured them to commit. These agencies planned to contact the students again to prevent their defection to other agencies.

However, the students that the finance secretariat telephoned were also wanted by other agencies such as MITI. The students had already visited the other agencies and gone home. Then the secretariat called and said: "The Ministry of Finance really wants to hire you. Please report as soon as possible." That night, the interested students arrived at the ministry. They were then detained and held there until the next day, being forced to stay overnight in the basement sleeping facilities. Reportedly among them were seven from MITI's secret list. Overall, eleven students were wanted by both the Ministry of Finance and MITI, but Finance reportedly won ten of them. Previously, desirable students had been shared in a more equitable fashion, say in a fifty-fifty or sixty-forty split. But in 1990, the Ministry of Finance ended up engineering a landslide recruitment victory. To make up for the loss, MITI stole recruits from other agencies such as Health and Welfare, Transport, and Posts and Telecommunications. These agencies that lost to MITI in turn stole students from other agencies. This chain reaction now repeats itself every year.

There was more to the Ministry of Finance's recruitment strategy than first meets the eye. The Ministry of Finance used to have the finest reputation among all the agencies, and even students who had been hired by other agencies would readily switch to the Ministry of Finance if given the chance. Other agencies had been compelled to devise measures to prevent the Ministry of Finance's "student swiping"; MITI, for instance, would detain students for a week at one of its training institutes outside Tokyo so as not to allow them to fall prey to the Ministry of Finance. Thus the Ministry of Finance's tactics in August 1990 can be seen as a response to a challenge. In any case, what is clear is that almost all the agencies routinely violate the agreements on recruitment. The Saturday of August 4, 1991 was more than two weeks before August 20, the day that students were officially allowed to visit prospective employers, and about one month before August 31, the day on which the final results of the Level I Entrance Examinations were to be released.

The agencies' "reception" practice is also questionable. According to an official who handles personnel, each agency sets aside several million yen of "reception money" to be spent on entertaining potential recruits at restaurants and bars. "Reception money" does not come out of the regular agency budget; agencies annually ask special interest groups for the money. An executive of a domestic-policy special interest group explained: "Every spring, interest-group executives get together and decide how much money to donate to the agencies. We tell government officials in charge of recruitment, 'please hire excellent students this year, as always,' and give them money." Not surprisingly, the Ministry of Finance and MITI reportedly collect much more "reception money" than other agencies.

Until recently, agencies kept a low profile in their "reception offensives." The feeling was that if a student who was admitted to the National Police Agency, for instance, were to tell his college classmates that he had been treated to fancy meals and drinks, that information would quickly reach all the personnel offices in Kasumigaseki. As a result, the student would be dropped by the National Police Agency. However, expensive "reception offensives" are now common practice.

The successful candidates for the Level I Entrance Examination are ranked according to their scores. However, this ranking is all but irrelevant to recruitment officials because the agencies have already compiled lists of desirable students long before the exam. A former personnel officer at the Ministry of Home Affairs stated: "The Level I Entrance Examination doesn't really measure what a candidate can do at work. I don't take the exam results into account at all in recruitment." There have actually been cases where an agency was not able to hire a student on its list because the student had subsequently failed the entrance examination.

Conversely, even a University of Tokyo law student who got the best score on the Level I Entrance Examination might not be admitted to the agency of his choice. About six years ago, the student with the highest score ended up in an agency that was not his first choice. He commented: "I visited a ministry I was interested in but was told that interviews were by appointment only. I felt betrayed. Then I visited the agency that I now work for and was hired on the spot."

What matters most to agencies about the applicant? Personnel officers pay closest attention not to a student's entrance examination score but his or her junior year grades at the University of Tokyo Law Department, as well as his or her reputation within the department. The student mentioned above was about one hundredth in ranking in terms of grades in the Law Department, rendering him less desirable in the eyes of his first choice agency. In point of fact, though, not all the recruits hired by the Ministry of Finance and Ministry of Home Affairs are in the "academically superior" category.

Ministry Prestige Determined by Recruits

Although agencies do hire students from departments other than law and economics at the University of Tokyo, as well as from other colleges, these students are a low priority for the agencies. Agencies, in particular the Ministry of Finance and Ministry of Home Affairs, do everything possible to hire University of Tokyo Law Department students whose grades are near the top of their class. A high official at the Ministry of Finance explains that "to maintain the ministry's prestige and ability to guide the increasingly powerful financial industry, we must hire students who are academically superior to those at other agencies." A Ministry of Home Affairs official echoes this sentiment: "Our ministry would not get respect from prefectural governments and other national agencies if our recruits pale academically in comparison to theirs." In other words, to be in control, government agencies need to construct and maintain an image of being comprised of "the best and the brightest." Having legally authorized power is not enough.

Oddly enough, many University of Tokyo Law Department recruits are not always stellar performers, and both ministries have recently begun to pursue a policy of hiring students who actually seem capable of doing the job. The "tug of war" among agencies has now become a fight over a mere thirty or forty University of Tokyo law students. Securing these students with the best grades is believed to symbolize a ministry's prestige.

However, even Todai law students who are not from the top of their class will be hired, because, as a personnel officer at an economic agency explained: "The media widely publicizes which agencies hire how many University of Tokyo Law Department graduates. That's why we must hire as many the other agencies do." As a result of this policy, agencies have run into trouble when they hire a Todai law graduate that turns out to be incompetent or inept.

As one may gather from the above, the myth of the University of Tokyo Law Department and the agencies' scramble for Todai recruits has become ludicrous. Still, it will probably not be debunked anytime soon. Interministry ranking is decided upon the basis of the number of top law students hired, not on the basis of what function the ministries perform or what legal place they have in the government.

The legal ranking of the ministries, which incidentally is also the seating order at administrative vice-minister meetings, is as follows:

1. Ministry of Justice
2. Ministry of Foreign Affairs
3. Ministry of Finance
4. Ministry of Education
5. Ministry of Health and Welfare
6. Ministry of Agriculture, Forestry, and Fisheries
7. MITI
8. Ministry of Transport
9. Ministry of Posts and Telecommunications
10. Ministry of Labor
11. Ministry of Construction
12. Ministry of Home Affairs

While the number of University of Tokyo recruits per agency has nothing to do with this legal ranking, an unwritten hierarchy of the interministry top four, based on the number of University of Tokyo graduates hired by each, exists. This hierarchy is as follows (excluding the Ministry of Foreign Affairs, which administers its own Diplomatic Service Examination):

1. Ministry of Finance
2. MITI

3. Ministry of Home Affairs
4. National Police Agency

These four are often called the "Four Dynasties." According to the 1990 recruitment records for Todai graduates, the Ministry of Finance was ranked at the top, and the Ministry of Home Affairs was second, with MITI and the National Police Agency under them.

After the "Four Dynasties" the second grouping in the unwritten hierarchy, is composed of economic agencies:

5. Ministry of Posts and Telecommunications
6. Ministry of Transport
7. Ministry of Construction
8. Ministry of Agriculture, Forestry, and Fisheries
9. Ministry of Health and Welfare

This group is followed by a third group:

10. Ministry of Labor
11. Ministry of Education
12. Ministry of Justice

Agencies that have recently become popular with students, such as the Economic Planning Agency and the Environment Agency, would now probably be located somewhere between the second and the third groups. Decreasing in popularity are the Prime Minister's Office and the Management and Coordination Agency, both of which lose students to other agencies every year.

This unwritten hierarchy, however, is changing slowly but surely. Among the economic agencies, the Ministry of Construction and the Ministry of Agriculture, Forestry, and Fisheries have remained relatively stable in the hierarchy. The Ministry of Construction, in particular, is considered the best place for technology officials to work. On the other hand, the ranking of the Ministry of Transport and Ministry of Posts and Telecommunications has been changing drastically. The Ministry of Transport somehow has become increasingly popular with students since the ministry's aviation administration became an issue in the Lockheed scandal in the 1970s. The Ministry of Posts and Telecommunications has been rapidly moving up in the hierarchy in recent years, and, as an economic agency, it now follows directly behind MITI. The development of information and communications technologies, and the ministry's victory over MITI in a struggle for control of the VAN, or Value-Added Network (a business communications network) has increased its popularity with students.

The Ministry of Labor and Ministry of Education are also changing. Both ministries had been responsible for overseeing the recruitment agreements among agencies, and therefore refrained from making contacts with students before the day the ban was lifted each year. Now both ministries openly violate the recruitment agreements. In 1990, applicants from the University of Tokyo to the Ministry of Education reportedly increased by 50 percent over the previous year.

Bureaucratic Careers Plummet in Popularity

In early August of 1990, I had an opportunity to speak with ten seniors at the University of Tokyo Law Department and Economics Department. Following are highlights of their views:

- The popularity of the economic agencies has peaked. Several students essentially stated: "The age of materialism and money is over; from now on people and culture are what counts."
- Many students want to avoid strong, traditionally authoritative agencies such as the Ministry of Finance and the National Police. The rising popularity of the Economic Planning Agency and Environment Agency reflects this desire.
- An increasing number of students, particularly those in the Economics Department, want to "concentrate on one type of work rather than becoming a generalist."

On the whole, I was astonished by what the students had to say. Several students expressed a common sentiment, that working for large trading companies such as Mitsui & Co. and Mitsubishi International had little appeal to them because it does not take a great deal of brains to work for such companies. Among private sector jobs, the Industrial Bank of Japan and the planning section of a major bank in Tokyo would be acceptable because they require a lot of intelligence.

Having passed brutal entrance exams, University of Tokyo students have been taught to define their lives according to such crucial tests, and they appear to consider test scores as the yardstick by which to measure job desirability. Difficult entrance tests are a sign that a job is desirable; their own interests, talents, and special skills, or the profession's value to society seem irrelevant. As long as the examinations for a profession are difficult and challenging, it "looks good," and these students will want to enter that profession. Passing the Level I Entrance Examination or the National Bar Exam looks good on resumes.

University of Tokyo Law Department students have a different perspective compared with other students aspiring to become national public servants. Most students from other universities have concrete reasons as well as a sense of purpose in wanting to become bureaucrats:

"I want to help accelerate technological development."
— *an economics major*

"I want to go into space research and development."
— *a communications technology student*

"Outlying localities are the key to Japan's development in the twenty-first century. I want to help them grow."
— *an economics major*

"I am interested in broadcast administration."
— *an electronics major*

"I am interested in environmental protection."
— *a landscape planning student*

In contrast, many University of Tokyo law students do not seem nearly as open-minded. Interested only in promotion, some even conduct extensive research on the personnel policy of a prospective agency. They are interested in nothing else. Investigation reveals that this attitude is quite common among them. One cannot help wondering about the kind of public administration these students would carry out when they became bureaucrats. Despite their lack of purpose, government agencies still attempt to recruit as many Todai law students as possible. A high-ranking transport official stated: "Recent new recruits are very capable. About ten years ago, there used to be some director-generals who were rather a disgrace to the Ministry of Transport. Now any new University of Tokyo recruit is a fine candidate for future director-general. They are studious, shrewd, and irreproachable."

University of Tokyo students who aspire to be bureaucrats are indeed considered "irreproachable." About twenty years ago, every now and then brilliant students from rural public schools were admitted to the University of Tokyo Law Department and went on to become bureaucrats. But today, it is rare for these unique students to succeed in the competitive process of entrance examinations. As stated at the beginning of this chapter, the majority of successful students come from well-to-do families that can afford to send their children to urban and suburban schools that are known for forwarding their graduates to the University of Tokyo. As a result, most career bureaucrats overwhelmingly come from wealthy families in either the Tokyo or Osaka metropolitan region.

To illustrate the problem of lopsided demographic representation in the bureaucracy, the number of new officials at the Ministry of Agriculture, Forestry, and Fisheries who have never seen rice paddies is on the rise. In an attempt to compensate for their inexperience, the ministry sends many of its second-year career bureaucrats to family farms and fishing villages for thirty days of training. This practice would have been unthinkable ten years ago. But if the ministry hired more students who were truly familiar with agriculture instead of University of Tokyo Law Department graduates, the ministry's position in the unwritten hierarchy would sink, and it can little afford a loss in reputation. The thirty-day annual visit to farm and fishing communities, then, strikes a compromise.

The interagency struggle over University of Tokyo Law Department students reveals the bureaucracy's exaggerated sense of self-importance and a high degree of stupidity. Doing things the established way and at any cost is nothing new in Kasumigaseki. Ignoring a prime minister's injunction seems to trouble no bureaucrat.

4

DISILLUSIONED WITH THE SYSTEM

Institutionalized Inefficiency

Anyone who rides in a taxi past Kasumigaseki at midnight would be surprised to find that nearly all the windows of the government buildings are lit. This is especially the case if you visit around the end of the year or during a Diet session. At three or four in the morning, taxis line up in front of the National Personnel Authority and the Ministry of Finance, waiting to be hailed by bureaucrats.

During an interview, a taxi driver who works the late shift in the Kasumigaseki district described significant behavioral differences between the ordinary *sarariman* and the bureaucrat: "I seldom witness officials in a drunken state. Nor have I ever seen an official doze off in my taxi. Most of my passengers are bureaucrats of about the age of thirty. They say little. Once they get in the taxi, they keep quiet and stare out the window."

In another interview, Nakajima Yoshio, the private secretary to the prime minister, recalled his earlier days at the Budget Bureau: "The Budget Bureau is extremely busy from September to December. I would usually go home around three or four in the morning. Since my wife would be asleep at that time, I would either drink beer alone or take a quiet bath if I had the energy for it. A few hours later, I would have breakfast and reach the office by 9:30 in the morning. But I would be especially careful not to make any noise because some of my subordinates stayed at the office overnight and would still be sleeping."

A former Ministry of Finance bureaucrat, who is at present a branch office manager of a major Japanese bank, expressed the following skepticism over the typical work habits in the bureaucracy: "There must be a change in the way national budgets are planned. A prefecture in northeastern Japan made an adjustment in their budget-making procedures so that its Finance Bureau people did not have to work late into the night. While the Diet is in session, all government agencies stay open until early morning, but there is no real necessity to do so. Even if the Diet poses bombshell questions, bureaucrats should not have to worry if they are truly capable and self-confident."

Also of interest are the views of Sabashi Shigeru, a former administrative vice-minister of MITI, who was later the model for a character in the popular novel *The Summer of the Bureaucrats*. In his own book *An Unusual Bureaucrat*, he states:

> The government's budget assessment system is simply one of the most wasteful processes in Japan. Who knows what it takes to keep the system running: how many officials are needed, how many hours are spent, how high are the costs of preparing written materials and of mobilizing special interests, and so on and on? I would say the system probably costs billions of yen. Year after year the system repeats itself, yet nobody complains.
>
> In late December every year, the lights at the Ministry of Finance's Budget Bureau are on all night long, and the newspapers print photos of the lighted building as though a metaphor for the government officials' selfless and diligent work. Though exhausted, the Budget Bureau people enjoy an ego trip from the process.

Indeed, in Kasumigaseki, work hours tend to be irregular year round, and an incredible amount of overtime is put in. An agency responsible for taking on important tasks may provide an incredibly hectic environment. Kato Ryozo, a former high-ranking official for the Ministry of Foreign Affairs, gives testimony to this: "In November 1990, when the Persian Gulf Crisis coincided with Emperor Akihito's coronation ceremony, we were extremely busy at the Ministry of Foreign Affairs. That month, two officials put in three hundred hours of overtime, and fifteen officials put in more than two hundred hours." Apparently budget making and responding to the Diet are not the only sources of bureaucratic anxiety and overwork.

However, some departments in the bureaucracy are less pressed than others, because they have much less work to do, yet, the officials of those departments must work to maintain a semblance of industriousness. A mid-level bureaucrat at a certain unnameable ministry confided: "A friend of mine who happens to be a section chief actually had little work to do but felt he couldn't go home because the other section chiefs around him stayed late at work. So my friend thought of a scheme to get out of this embarrassing situation: he decided that he would keep two jackets at work, one on his chair and one in his locker. He would leave one jacket on the chair, a fountain pen on his desk, and the desk light on. Then he would put on the jacket in his locker and leave the building to have a few drinks. Later he would return to the office to wrap up."

Behind Kasumigaseki's excessive use of overtime lies a pervading inefficiency. This inefficiency is in turn caused by a lack of coordination and unity among the agencies, whether on budget making or responding to the Diet. Unfortunately any sweeping reform is practically impossible for a number of reasons. For example, personnel transfer between agencies is strictly restricted, and an agency or division that occasionally needs extra help cannot get it. Another factor is that the Labor Standards Act, which restricts regular working hours and provides for overtime pay, does not apply to national government officials, and the cost of overtime does not prevent wasteful work as it would in the private sector. The above mentioned inflexibility in terms of personnel transfers is so extreme that it even applies to transfers within the same agency. An economic official complained: "In my office I was so busy that I wanted people from a different office within the same division to help me, but the division chief was no help.

I finally persuaded him to give his approval, talked to the Private Secretarial Division, and then obtained permission from the secretarial division chief. In the end, after all this effort, I succeeded in getting only two extra people to assist me."

Ironically, a number of government agencies, specifically the Ministry of Labor, MITI, and the Economic Planning Agency, are making efforts to shorten working hours in the private sector. The Ministry of Labor is pushing for an amendment of the Labor Standards Act. If this is implemented, a forty-hour work week and a rise in the national minimum wage would be possible. But how can the private sector be persuaded to shorten employee work hours when government officials set the opposite example by stubbornly adhering to wasteful and inefficient work habits? While the issue of work hours may not seem like a big issue, it symbolizes the problems Kasumi-gaseki faces.

High Expectations of "Super Elite" Bureaucrats

The Japanese public imagination is dominated by two contradictory images of its government officials. One is the image of the "corrupt bureaucrat," that is, the career official safely entrenched in the high tower of privilege and out of touch with society. Working in an administration that does not think of the "little people," these bureaucrats engage in interministry competition for government funds, licensing, and rigged bidding, and simply are the "root of all evil." In extreme contrast is the image of the "brilliant, super-intellectual bureaucrat." An academically-gifted genius, the super bureaucrat excels in selflessly serving the nation.

One question that comes to mind is why the Japanese public tolerates the corrupt bureaucrats. Why do they not criticize them and force them to change or else quit? As a matter of fact, in recent years the Japanese media has been endlessly and continuously criticizing its government officials and the bureaucratic system to a degree probably not paralleled in other industrialized nations. (Perhaps one reason the recent media barrage is so harsh is that during Japan's rapid postwar economic development, efforts to reform the bureaucracy were voluntarily restrained.) Both Gotoda Masaharu, former director-general of the National Police Agency, and Konaga Keiichi, former administrative vice-minister of MITI, have pointed out that the public's attitude toward the bureaucracy is somewhat contradictory. The Japanese people and the media, they say, complain about bureaucratic corruption and inefficiency, but when there are minor problems of the kind that in the U.S. would be taken care of by individuals or the private sector, the Japanese people expect the bureaucrats to be able to do something about them.

It is certainly true that the Japanese people exhibit a heavy dependence on the bureaucracy. Evidence of this attitude includes the numerous articles about government announcements that fill the front pages of Japan's major national newspapers. Also, while business leaders are prone to harshly criticize bureaucrats, they are humble and polite when meeting face to face with their ostensible enemy, even if the bureaucrat is far younger in age. A sort of blind, superficial, and child-like reverence characterizes the Japanese public's interaction with bureaucrats. But, the ultimate question is, can these very bureaucrats do the job they are expected to do? In answer to this, Japanese logic holds that since the bureaucrats were the most brilliant students to emerge from the educational system, they should not only be able to do their job, but to lead the country.

As mentioned earlier, in Japan only those who have scored extremely well on the college entrance examinations, especially those from the prestigious University of Tokyo, become top bureaucrats. Exactly how brilliant are these students? The Japanese novelist Oda Makoto, who attended the University of Tokyo, recalls some of them in an essay entitled "The Super-Brilliant Elites and the Ordinary Geniuses."

> Take for example learning foreign languages such as German or French. I know from first hand encounters with the super-brilliant elites that they already knew a smattering of those languages when they were still in high school. Even if they had not, they did so well in those subjects in college because they were memorization machines. They did well even if they did not want to. It was not uncommon for those elite students to do much better in French than those students who were pursuing a career in French literature.

A friend of mine, who later became a well-known novelist, related that the most brilliant student of French in his class at the University of Tokyo was a man who later became a high official. Years later, my friend ran into this former classmate, who by that time had forgotten almost all the French he learned in college. Nevertheless, he said that the practice of memorizing French had stood him in good stead, for it helped him to memorize overnight all the data necessary for answering questions at a Diet session.

When one takes a look at the textbooks belonging to those super-elite, one would mistake them for being brand new. They contain no underlining, no notes, nothing. Those students understood everything just by looking at the page.

Academic standards at the University of Tokyo may be high, but that does not mean that the students are well-rounded individuals. A Ministry of Foreign Affairs official had this opinion: "Japanese officials are weak because they have been sheltered. Most of them were outstanding students, but they have never experienced any major hardship. In contrast, officials in countries such as France, Germany, and Britain, where there are frequent shifts of political power, are tough, tenacious and unflappable. And they are able to maintain a clear distinction between politics and the bureaucracy."

From my many years as a Kasumigaseki watcher, I can say that Japan's high officials are a far cry from the toughness of their European counterparts. Scorned on the one hand as "corrupt bureaucrats" and idolized on the other as "brilliant super intellectuals," they have become demoralized, and, as we shall soon see, defeatism is spreading among the ministries.

Winners and Losers

An important difference between personnel management in the bureaucracy and the private sector is that in the bureaucracy, seniority is valued above all other factors. In the bureaucracy, unlike the private sector, one can never be promoted above a fellow official who entered one's agency in an earlier year. This is true no matter how capable the junior official when compared to the senior official.

Promotion protocol within the bureaucracy includes the following:

- Elite bureaucrats, or *kanryo*, do not stay in a post very long: in general, the maximum is two years at one position. Delegating responsibility for day-to-day affairs to non-career officials and technology officials, elite bureaucrats move from one post to another as generalists. They rarely become specialists, whether in labor, business, or finance, as is common in the private sector. Specialization is never a factor in career advancement.

- Non-career and technology officials are evaluated on a regular basis. In compliance with National Personnel Authority Rule 10-2, all the agencies evaluate their officials who rank at or below division chief. However, non-career officials and technology officials in particular are the main focus of evaluation. Career, or elite, bureaucrats are hardly affected by the National Personnel Authority rule.

- The most important consideration for an elite bureaucrat's career is a work history that records transitions every year or two from one post to another. Every level, from the lowest position to manager, from section chief, to division chief, to department head and soon, up to director-general of a bureau, is assigned a specific ranking. One's work history clearly depicts how one measures up to others who joined the agency at the same time. In the majority of agencies, these work histories typically are the only records kept by the personnel section on a bureaucrat's career. One exception to this rule is the Ministry of Finance, which reportedly documents comments from people outside the ministry on its career officials.

How then, are career bureaucrats assigned and promoted to positions? A former MITI administrative vice-minister explains: "Personnel management of bureaucrats can be summed up in one word: reputation. I can say from experience that reputation has been the best measurement by which personnel decisions are made." If one asks for a bureaucrat's reputation among his superiors, subordinates, same-year entrants, and outside people (including industry representatives concerned, LDP members, officials at other agencies, the media, and so on), that person's ranking among others who entered the agency in the same year becomes clear.

To base a career in the government solely on reputation does sound rather simplistic and subjective. In reality, most bureaucrats think their careers depend on luck and the ability of their assigned superiors. Supporting this notion is the fact that all career bureaucrats are more or less survivors of extremely tough entrance examinations and do not differ much in academic and administrative abilities. If given the opportunity, they would perform well in any position and move on to the next. However, there is a limit to the number of next-level positions available to same-year entrants. Therefore, if a bureaucrat earned a good post early in his career, he would rank above same-year colleagues. On the other hand, if one failed to gain a good position early on, one would remain at a relatively lower ranking. It is widely known that having a supportive superior is critical, because the superior's "favors" assist a bureaucratic career. In several agencies, examples abound of superior-subordinate combinations repeating upwards several times over.

Such bureaucratic personnel management practices have remained unchanged since the founding of the modern Japanese bureaucratic system during the Meiji Restoration. If anything, these practices have become even more rigid. For instance, there used to be more second chances for bureaucrats who missed out on valuable promotions early in their career. Nowadays, a bureaucrat's career path is rigidly predetermined by the promotion system as described above. This has a great deal to do with the bureaucracy becoming more and more inward-looking as the private sector has come to be able to take care of itself. Not only have the agencies' battles for turf intensified, but so too the bureaucrats' battles for high-ranking posts. To help settle personnel management matters, other agencies have adapted, with limited success, the Ministry of Finance's more severe practices, which are described below. While the Ministry of Finance has learned to manage its employees though years of experience, even it is having difficulty keeping up with the changing attitudes of younger officials.

Some career bureaucrats who start out with what it takes to become administrative vice-minister or director-general of an agency are eliminated from that track within ten years or so. Though this practice may seem brutal, it is done at all the agencies. At MITI, a bureaucrat's future depends almost entirely upon being selected a member of the Policy Planning Committee within twelve or thirteen years into one's career in the agency. Almost all career officials manage to become division chief, but it would be virtually impossible to make director-general or higher if one failed to become a member of the Ordinance Examination Committee.

The Ministry of Finance enacts this "first round of elimination" much earlier. Career bureaucrats first become local Tax Bureau chiefs after six or seven years, and by their eighth year, they return to the Ministry of Finance with a ranking equivalent to assistant division chief. In another two or three years, or at roughly thirty years of age, career officials are divided into either the "winner" or "loser" categories. On the other hand, future administrative vice-ministers and important director-generals are reportedly selected as soon as they enter the Ministry of Finance and then assigned to prestigious sections such as the Documents Section, the Secretariat Division of the Minister's Secretariat, or the Coordination Division of the Budget Bureau.

Seeking to avoid the demoralization that inevitably follows such non-objective promotion practices, the Ministry of Home Affairs assigns officials to divisions according to alphabetical order, but their example is a rare exception. Almost all agencies have been heading in the direction of earlier and earlier promotion decisions. Tracking of career officials has become more obviously a demoralizing waste of human resources, with negative and often destructive results.

Negative Consequences of Rigid Tracking

The problems of bureaucratic personnel management, particularly of those bureaucrats whose prospects for career advancement were doomed from the start, may be likened to "an accident waiting to happen." The sharp rise in the number of bureaucrats in their twenties or thirties who are fleeing from Kasumigaseki in droves indicates the magnitude of the problem. Some officials at the level of division chief lose hope for advancement, become disheartened, and abandon their responsibilities. At agencies where technical experts dominate, most top-level generalist officials do nothing other than act as human rubber stamps for documents that the technocrats produce.

Even bureaucrats who are on the elite career track can experience difficulties. Because of the early elimination process and the intense competition to get ahead, many bureaucrats are exhausted while in their late twenties. According to a law professor at the University of Tokyo: "My former students who become bureaucrats are able to talk only about their jobs after two or three years. It is a shame because they were much more well-rounded when they were students, before they entered the bureaucracy." Few in Kasumigaseki would dispute the validity of this statement.

In any case, being assigned under capable superiors, along with luck, is the key to a successful bureaucratic career. To gain the approval of a superior, one must be outstanding. However, the individual discretion that bureaucrats are allowed in doing their work has become more and more limited, and fewer opportunities are available to prove oneself through the quality of one's work alone. And job descriptions are becoming narrower and more rigid. It is common knowledge in Kasumigaseki, for example, that a director-general at the Ministry of Finance's Budget Bureau today performs at the level of a Budget Bureau general inspector of yesteryear. At present, the bureaucracy is trying to follow the rules laid out ten or twenty years ago, and routine work remains the mainstay. Quality projects such as planning bold policies or writing important legislation are few.

In such an environment, quantity becomes more important than quality in the bureaucratic mind set. Some officials try to impress their superiors by the sheer volume of their work. A telling episode is one in which a high official in an economic agency ordered some written material from a division chief in preparation for a visit from a foreign dignitary. This division chief in turn pushed his subordinates to produce a one-hundred page report. Upon receiving the report, the high official was flabbergasted: he actually had needed only two or three pages. In another example, an official brought back the subsidies his predecessor had struggled to eliminate, indicating a lack of an articulate agency policy. Some officials have made up projects for their agency that had no particular goal other than that of getting more money. Needless to say, such practices are nothing but a waste of tax revenue.

Bureaucratic apple-polishing has also gone too far. More officials than ever pay visits to officials at their agency's secretariat for no good reason other than to exchange pleasantries. Get-togethers under the name of "study groups" are also frequent: officials meet at restaurants or bars to establish personal contacts, or meetings are held by same-year entrants who have managed to get on the elite course. Even elite bureaucrats of different years arrange to meet in groups. Some bureaucrats make a point of getting invited to as many study group meetings as possible. These meetings take place in lavish reception halls and restaurants, and expenses are often paid by industries and special interest groups.

Considering such circumstances, does Japan's bureaucracy have the ability to solve its personnel problems by itself? A former administrative vice-minister at the Ministry of Home Affairs says, "It is not that politicians have assumed control of the bureaucracy's personnel management; rather, the bureaucracy, like some religious organizations, plays its own power games behind closed doors." It is hard to imagine that the winners behind these closed doors would voluntarily give up their privileges. At Kasumigaseki, the handful who have been triumphant in the power game carry on, while the rest are left behind.

The Escapees

One indication of the widespread demoralization in the bureaucracy is the high number of top officials who have quit the system. For what reasons have they abandoned their promising careers? To help answer this question, I attempted to interview twenty former high officials with backgrounds in law.

- Eight out of twenty declined to be interviewed.

- Of the remainder, five have entered the legal profession, five are in the private sector, one became an LDP Diet member, and one entered medical school.
- Year they entered government agencies: four during 1965–74; six during 1975–84; two after 1985.

Reasons for quitting after two to three years in an agency:

"I realized that I had chosen the wrong career."
—assistant judge who entered an agency in 1985

"Passing the Bar Exam was what I was really after."
—ex-bureaucrat who entered an agency in 1984

"It is hard to describe exactly why I quit. I guess the bureaucracy wasn't my kind of place."
—lawyer who entered an agency in 1976

Reasons for switching careers:

"I did not want to be an irrelevant part of the organization."

"I could not do any work that valued my initiative."

"The bureaucracy is so group-oriented that individuals accomplish little. I always wanted to help others, and I decided to choose a career that lets me help society on my own."
—medical student who entered an agency in 1980

"A lawyer would be rewarded by his clients for working hard to represent their interests, but an official gets no such feedback. People respect him not because of what he does but because of what he is."
—lawyer who entered an agency in 1976

"A career in the bureaucracy does not last long enough, especially if one expects to live to eighty years of age."

"I would not enjoy working in the private sector under *amakudari*."

"They say a career in the bureaucracy is stable, but most bureaucrats are compelled to quit after twenty-five years or so for one reason or another. It's very demoralizing to be forced to leave your career while still in your forties. You cannot function outside an organization when you have become used to it."

—lawyer who entered an agency in 1982

"I felt sorry for a friend of mine who had to do *amakudari* while in his forties. He said that he received good treatment on paper, but actually there was not much work to do."

—manufacturing executive who entered an agency in 1970

"Dissatisfaction with pay and benefits."

"Work is no longer fun because government is not that important."

"Political considerations have become so vital and pervasive that bureaucrats have less discretion than ever."

"When I was in the bureaucracy, I was so busy that I could not spend much time with my family. Budget making and Diet sessions forced me to work late ridiculously often. It was silly."

—hotel owner who entered an agency in 1977

"While it does have its own rewards, the bureaucracy has become more and more interested in getting a bigger share of the economic pie for itself and the industries it supervises. Japan has become so developed a nation that it needs less and less government help. It didn't make sense to me to spend so much energy and resources to go after a bigger share of the pie."

—construction executive who entered an agency in 1968

"Whenever we tried to do something, other agencies would complain and everything would get compromised. Besides, we had to devote ourselves to maintaining the status quo, and there was no room for creativity."

—lawyer who had entered an agency in 1982

"I was transferred too frequently from one post to another in different regions."

"I took up a job in an agency not because I really wanted to but because I was compelled to follow in my father's footsteps."

"Bureaucrats' work habits are extremely inefficient."

Finally, it is worth noting that most expressed personal reasons rather than complaints about the system itself such as pay or work content. Despite this, even incumbent officials in Kasumigaseki consider personnel management to be a serious issue in the bureaucracy. Second chances for those who fail to gain admission onto the elite track are becoming increasingly rare, leading one ex-bureaucrat in the above group to complain that "future prospects were grim."

Discontent Even Among the Winners

Surprisingly, more often than not even those who are supposedly the winners in the system and have remained inside it, people who have attained the rank of administrative vice-minister, director-general, or director-general of the secretariat, are the first to express frustrations with Kasumigaseki:

"If I could go back in time, I would not have chosen to become a bureaucrat. Things are totally different now from what they were thirty years ago. Divisiveness within the bureaucracy is out of hand. The distinction between politics and public administration has blurred. Open discussions, which were once the major appeal of bureaucracy, are no more."
                    —*director-general of an economic agency*

"As one moves up in the bureaucracy, one has to devote more and more time to outside, non-official work, for example, attending funerals and weddings. We cannot work conscientiously. I doubt that there is any meaning in the life of a bureaucrat."
                    —*director-general of the secretariat at an adjustment agency*

"There is such a thing as fate. The neighbor's grass is always greener, but when fate makes you a bureaucrat, you have to live with it. When a legislator ridicules you at a Diet session or talks as though bureaucrats are the root of all evil, you can do nothing but think of it as your fate."

—councillor at an economic agency

"Government officials are much less personable than they used to be. When I first became a bureaucrat, we were able to create policy for policy's sake. Now we must spend a great deal of time accommodating Diet members' and special interest groups' demands. We are no longer adhering to the ethical standards that we are supposed to be upholding."

—director-general at an adjustment agency

The Suicide of a High Official

Similar frustrations have intensified in Kasumigaseki since the time of the 1990 Persian Gulf Crisis. Then, on December 5, 1990, came the suicide of Yamauchi Toyonori, then head of the Planning and Coordination Bureau at the Environment Agency, which was a great blow to morale. Yamauchi's death came as a surprise to most bureaucrats because suicides of high-ranking officials do not happen every day. There had been two suicides of incumbent officials of equivalent rank: the head of the Defense Agency Equipment Bureau who had formerly been a MITI official, and a National Police Academy superintendent who had formerly been director of the Osaka City Police. But while both of these suicides shocked bureaucrats, they were publicly attributed to "personal problems." Other possible factors, such as a destructive work environment, were not investigated.

The response to Yamauchi's suicide, however, was markedly different; many bureaucrats felt it to be the direct result of structural problems within the bureaucracy. To be sure, academic studies of suicide tend to avoid attributing the cause to external factors such as problems at work. Nevertheless, many bureaucrats strongly suspected that the bureaucracy's internal structure was enough to drive Yamauchi to suicide. One might ask, what structural problems are severe enough to provoke suicide? Before getting into that question, let us first examine the actual numbers of public officials as a whole who killed themselves, particularly the situation among career bureaucrats with a background in law.

Suicide Rate Higher than the Private Sector

Each year, the National Personnel Authority releases a report entitled "Leading Causes of Death and Mortality Rate Among National Officials, with Comparison to the Causes and Rates of the General Public." According to the 1989 report, 1,217 public officials died in the fiscal year 1988–89, out of a total number of 825,000 officials. The four main causes of death were, in order:

1. cancer (564 deaths)
2. coronary ailments (143)
3. stroke (124)
4. suicide (112)

The order of the leading causes of death among public officials is the same as that for the general public, and the order has not changed in recent years. The mortality rate, which is the number of deaths a year per 100,000 people, is 147.1 for officials, as compared to 256.5 for the rest of the population. The suicide rate is 13.6 for officials and 20.5 for the general public. What these figures boil down to is that in the population as a whole (including bureaucrats) 8 percent of deaths are attributable to suicide, whereas the corresponding figure for public officials alone is 9.2 percent.

The suicide rate of public officials also exceeds that of employees at major Japanese corporations, who presumably work under comparably stressful conditions: in 1984, the suicide rate was 15.9 for officials, and 13.4 for employees of major corporations. The suicide rate of officials in 1988 was 13.5 overall, but there was a sudden jump in the number of such suicides during part of that year. The following are the series of suicide rates of public officials in general over several previous years:

1979	11.1
1980	13.1
1981	12.6
1982	15.2
1983	17.5
1984	15.6
1985	15.9

The following are the suicide rates of public officials in their forties for the same years:

1979	10.2
1980	17.9
1981	9.9
1982	16.4
1983	21.8
1984	15.5
1985	19.9

As one can see from the figures given above, the suicide rate of public officials as a class peaked in 1983 and has since then remained at a high level. The increase in suicide rates among officials in their forties and fifties, namely those in management positions, is particularly noteworthy.

In 1982, when Nakasone Yasuhiro became prime minister, he embarked on reform of public administration and finance. Several major steps were taken by the Nakasone administration, including "zero ceiling" budget making (automatically securing the same budget allocation for an agency as in the previous year), privatizing the Japan National Railways (JNR) and the Nippon Telegraph and Telephone Public Corporation (NTT), and forming the Management and Coordination Agency by combining the Administrative Management Agency and certain functions of the Prime Minister's Office. As these steps were implemented, officials in management positions were placed under increasing stress, which may have been a factor behind the marked increase in the number of suicides in the bureaucracy in that and the following year. Afterwards, as prime ministers came and went and administrative reform receded somewhat as a public issue, suicide rates also seemed to decrease.

While government officials in general went through the same stressful conditions described above, what was happening to the elite officials, the career bureaucrats with backgrounds in law or economics? Precise figures on the suicides of high officials are difficult to come by, partly because of the issue of privacy. However, there is no question that there were high officials who committed suicide, even during the decade before Yamauchi's death. Here are some examples

Ministry of Finance: Two assistant division chiefs at the Securities Bureau, one official at the Budget Bureau, and one official on assignment at the National Tax administration Agency.

MITI: One division chief.

Ministry of Agriculture, Forestry, and Fisheries: One young official who had been at the agency for four or five years since being hired in 1980 or 1981.

National Police Agency: One National Police Academy Superintendent and one assistant division chief at the Criminal Investigation Bureau.

Ministry of Home Affairs: Two officials who entered in the mid-1970s (one of the two deaths may have been alcoholism-related).

Ministry of Health and Welfare: One official committed suicide in 1992 while on assignment in the Prime Minister's Office.

While precise comparisons are difficult, it is probably safe to assume that the suicide rate among high officials is even higher than that among public officials as a whole. Why, then, do high officials, people who have successfully survived "examination hell" and whose career prospects look very bright, commit suicide?

Victims of Party Politics

Suicides of career officials used to be attributed to corruption and exposure. But these days they are not. There are three points that many officials agree on. First, bureaucrats' work hours are too long. They are seldom able to take vacations. For example, the suicide of the assistant division chief at the National Police Agency was attributed by many to overwork because he killed himself shortly after he had performed intensive security duties for the Tokyo Summit meetings of the leaders of the seven industrial countries. Problems at home, such as divorce, are also much more common than in the private sector.

There also may be problems inherent in the type of work assigned to bureaucrats. An assistant division chief at the Ministry of Finance killed himself shortly after coming back from an overseas assignment. A young official at the Ministry of Home Affairs was found dead shortly after returning to Tokyo from duty in a rural area. Most bureaucrats have concluded the root of the problem with their work to be that the bureaucracy does not value creativity, and that many officials spend a ridiculous amount of time and energy coordinating among various agencies.

Suicides may also be attributed to the bureaucracy's practice of hiring officials on the sole basis of academic records. Not every career, or elite, bureaucrat can make the top positions of director-general or administrative vice-minister, and, as seen in the previous section, some agencies decide within the first ten years who will be in charge of a bureau or division, and who will not. Although those who miss out still move up much faster than non-career officials, they tend to be sorely disappointed, and possibly depressed, because never before have they experienced defeat in their lives.

As for Yamauchi, many observers felt that he was a casualty of the "LDP revered, politics despised" phenomenon, that is, the prevailing belief in Japan that, despite political mayhem and corruption, the LDP's methods are effective in getting things done. An LDP Diet member who had met Yamauchi two days before his suicide commented: "Mr.

Yamauchi seemed fine; he smiled a lot. But the LDP was cruel to him; the party never listened to him yet made demand after demand while he was trying to give serious thought to the issues. He was driven to the brink while trying to do good." Some bureaucrats think that the impossible demands of party politics may drive even more officials to commit suicide. Division chiefs and higher officials may be driven to kill themselves in frustration over trying to satisfy demands from all sides. This conflict is at the heart of the bureaucracy's structural problems.

One might ask, if work is so tough for officials, why don't they resign? That escape route does not really apply to bureaucrats. While one can resign with relative ease within the first five or six years after entering the bureaucracy, resignation after that grace period brands one a traitor to the organization. Furthermore, individual bureaucrats strongly feel that to resign declares oneself a loser. Fear of becoming a loser among one's peers compels bureaucrats to stay, even if they are unhappy with their work. This attitude seems to be bolstered by bureaucrats' personal pride in being members of the elites of society, a position of glory that is hard to relinquish. Indeed, the bureaucracy is a strange and closed society. The suicide of Yamauchi, then, poses a warning to the elitist bureaucracy.

5

ADMINISTRATION AT A STANDSTILL

Inside the Agencies

In this chapter I will attempt to shed some light on the inner workings of Kasumigaseki by taking a closer look at nine government agencies. Five of these are ministries: the Ministry of Finance, MITI, the Ministry of Foreign Affairs, the Ministry of Construction, and the Ministry of Transport. Two of the remaining four, the Public Prosecutors Office and the Immigration Bureau, are administrative divisions of the Ministry of Justice. Another, the National Police Agency, is under the National Public Safety Commission, which is in turn under the Prime Minister's Office. And finally, the Cabinet Legislation Bureau, with which I will begin, falls directly under the Cabinet in the organizational chart of the Japanese government's administrative branch.

The Cabinet Legislation Bureau: A Privileged Status

The Fourth Government Agency complex of Kasumigaseki is a white twelve-story building that is connected to the main building of the Ministry of Finance by a roofed passageway. The Cabinet Legislation

Bureau, occupying two-thirds of the building's eleventh floor, is a relatively small agency with a staff of seventy-six and a total annual budget of 750 million yen, salaries included (as of fiscal year 1992). Despite its small size, the Cabinet Legislation Bureau is regarded as an agency of special authority because it holds one of the two primary powers of the bureaucracy: the power to evaluate laws. The Ministry of Finance's Budget Bureau holds the other primary power, the power to make the national budget. The Cabinet Legislation Bureau had generally been regarded as perhaps the last bastion of the bureaucracy, and, until recently, was considered the only remaining agency immune from political influence.

In 1991, however, the Cabinet Legislation Bureau was rocked by the Persian Gulf War and the subsequent national debate over sending Japan's Self-Defense Forces aircraft to the gulf region to rescue refugees. Many in the government feared that a crisis similar to the 1973 Bank of Japan incident might threaten the bureau's credibility. In that incident, which occurred during the first oil crisis in 1973, Bank of Japan President Sasaki Tadashi conceded to political pressure from Prime Minister Tanaka Kakuei by slackening the bank's tight monetary policy, an action that caused inflation to skyrocket. The Bank of Japan incurred a permanent scar on its reputation.

Before examining the crisis in the bureaucracy that was created by the debate over sending units of the Self-Defense Forces to the Middle East, we need to understand what the Cabinet Legislation Bureau is all about.

Exclusive Authority. The forerunner of the present-day Cabinet Legislation Bureau was the Legislation Bureau, which was founded in 1885 as an organization under direct control of the Cabinet. Along with the Ministry of the Army, the Ministry of the Navy, the Home Ministry, and Ministry of Justice, the Legislation Bureau was abolished in 1948 by the authority of the Allied Occupation government. As the following anecdote illustrates, the Legislation Bureau had been extremely powerful.

When Tojo Hideki was serving as both prime minister and minister of the Army (1941–44), the Ministry of the Army submitted a plan for its own reorganization to the Legislation Bureau for approval. Although an Army Affairs official visited the Legislation Bureau counsellor on many occasions to plead for approval of the proposal, the latter kept witholding it. To alleviate the situation, a Ministry of the Army's director-general also called on the Legislation Bureau, but the bureau counsellor simply told him to "tell Minister Tojo to go commit suicide by *harakiri* for presenting us with such a problematic issue." Enraged, the Ministry of the Army leadership demanded that the Legislation Bureau fire this insubordinate counsellor. But the Legislation Bureau refused. Instead they attached their bureau counsellor's comment to the Army proposal and then forwarded it to the Tojo administration.

The former Legislation Bureau held three powers: to evaluate bills and treaties that the administration sent to the Diet, to evaluate the government's structure and adjust the number of employees per agency accordingly, and to administer the civil service examinations. Today, the Entrance Examinations for National Civil Service are administered by the National Personnel Authority, and government structural matters are supervised by the Management and Coordination Agency.

The Legislation Bureau also had a reputation for recruiting officials from other agencies who held the top ten scores in the National Civil Service Examination, Public Administration Category. Under the Meiji Constitution, bureaucrats were completely in charge of public administration, rendering the Diet relatively powerless. Even among the generally powerful bureaucracies, the Legislation Bureau was known to be a "bureaucracy that tops other bureaucracies." The Privy Council, which was the emperor's highest advisory board, was the only agency that could keep the Legislation Bureau in check.

The Legislation Bureau was dismantled by the Occupation government, but under Prime Minister Yoshida Shigeru a new Cabinet Legislation Bureau was created in 1952. Though stripped of its authority over the National Civil Service Examinations and the government's structure and of its power to adjust the number of employees per agency, the Cabinet Legislation Bureau, under the new Constitution of Japan would, as we will see, be conferred even greater power than its predecessor. Out of respect for the dismantled Legislation Bureau, the director-general of the Cabinet Legislation Bureau was designated a "special post," and its holder was paid a salary equivalent to that of the head of the Imperial Household Agency and the Federal Trade Commission (FTC) chairman. Under the Meiji Constitution, the Legislation Bureau director-general had been paid a higher salary than even the chief Cabinet secretary. Though the present Cabinet Legislation Bureau director-general's salary is not as great as it used to be, his salary is still considerably greater than the second-highest position at the Cabinet Secretariat, and the post carries with it an official residence (measuring 2,310 square meters) in the exclusive Jingumae district of Tokyo.

The Cabinet Legislation Bureau director-general is the only non-minister of state whose name is listed along with the names of the Cabinet members when a new administration is formed. Since he is not one of those officials whose appointment must be attested by the emperor, he does not attend the attestation ceremony. But in the commemorative photographs, he appears alongside the Cabinet members on the staircase within the Diet chamber, and he always attends Cabinet meetings. During the Diet Budget Committee meetings in which legislators ask the Cabinet questions not limited to matters of the budget, the Cabinet Legislation Bureau chief always sits directly behind the prime minister. Thus, the "Cabinet's legal counsel," is endowed with a privileged status.

How then did the revived Cabinet Legislation Bureau regain the former power of its predecessor? First, the postwar bureau was given broader authority to evaluate legislation and treaties than the old Legislation Bureau. Under the Meiji Constitution, as the Diet did not have much power, the government issued many imperial decrees not subject to Diet evaluation. An extreme example came in 1944, during World War II: while only 33 laws were established that year, an astonishing 677 imperial decrees were issued. Today, the current Constitution designates the Diet as the "highest organ of state power." Items that once were decided by imperial decree are now subject to Diet deliberation. Consequently, the number of laws has increased dramatically. At present, there are nearly 1,600 laws in the books, close to three times the number of laws that existed before the war. Moreover, the number of Cabinet orders rose to 1,720 in 1985.

The bureau has the authority of prior evaluation of all laws that the Cabinet submits to the Diet (these represent more than 80 percent of all laws) and all Cabinet orders. When compared to the old Legislation Bureau, which could not evaluate imperial decrees, this is a dramatic expansion of authority. Also, the Cabinet Legislation Bureau's authority extends to laws drawn up by the Ministry of Justice. Even if the Ministry of Justice obtains the backing of a Legislative Council for proposed amendments to criminal or civil laws, the ministry cannot send the proposal to a Cabinet meeting until it has been approved by the Cabinet Legislation Bureau.

Many bureaucrats find it far more stressful to report to the Cabinet Legislation Bureau than to report to the Ministry of Finance Budget Bureau. According to The Centennial History of the Cabinet Legislation Bureau: "[The bureau] evaluates a bill and its relationship to the Constitution and to other laws currently in effect; examines the precision and accuracy of the language in conveying the bill's intent, the order of clauses, and the appropriateness of wording; and evaluates these aspects of the bill from every legal and technical angle, covering everything from the title, the table of contents, general clauses, sections to the very impetus for writing the bill."

The evaluation is first undertaken by the bureau's counsellors, all of whom are on temporary assignment from other agencies, after which the bill is checked by the appropriate department head, the deputy director-general, and then the director-general of the Cabinet Legislation Bureau. After being approved by these officials, the bill can then be forwarded to a Cabinet meeting. During this evaluation period, many bills are drastically amended or even rejected. No agency reportedly has ever had a Cabinet order proposal forwarded to a Cabinet meeting in its original form. In effect, the bill's relationship to the Constitution and to current laws are the points most closely scrutinized. Many bills have to be rewritten after being deemed in violation of either the constitutional clause that "every person shall have freedom to choose and change his residence and to choose his occupation to the extent that it does not interfere with the public welfare"(Article 22) or the clause that "the right to hold property is inviolable"(Article 29). The Large-scale Retail Stores Law and the Land Expropriation Law are examples of bills revised because found unconstitutional by the Cabinet Legislation Bureau.

A second important power that the postwar bureau has acquired in addition to that of approving laws is a de facto authority to interpret the constitutionality of laws. Until the end of World War II, only a few constitutional issues had been debated in the Diet, for example, the Total National Mobilization Law of 1938. However, in the postwar Diet, Article 9 of the new Constitution has come up repeatedly in connection with national defense and foreign policy issues, and the interpretation of constitutionality has been an issue in other key legislation. Consequently, the Cabinet Legislation Bureau's director-general and chief of its First Department have been questioned many times at Diet sessions, and this fact has further validated the authority of the bureau's interpretation of the constitutionality of laws. Of course, as Article 81 of the Constitution states, "The Supreme Court is the court of last resort with power to determine the constitutionality of any law, order, regulation or official act." But the Supreme Court has rarely exercised this power of judicial review; the court has declared only five laws unconstitutional, one example being a case involving unequal representation in the lower house of the Diet due to flawed districting.

In fact, the constitutionality of laws and Cabinet orders representing more than 80 percent of all legislation are evaluated solely by the Cabinet Legislation Bureau, leading many to call it the "de facto constitutional court." Its interpretations of administrative law are almost always accepted by the courts because they are based on both practical considerations and specialist knowledge. The powers of the Cabinet Legislation Bureau are certainly no less than those of its predecessor.

Appointing Brilliant Officials from Other Agencies. The Cabinet Legislation Bureau has proven to be an attractive destination for officials on temporary assignment from other agencies. It has four departments and an administration office. The bureau's second in command, or deputy director-general, is of the same rank as an administrative vice-minister at other agencies. Also, a Cabinet Legislation Bureau department head is a rank equivalent to bureau chief, or director-general, of other agencies. The First Department is the most powerful and is called the "Opinion Department," as it is responsible for judging the constitutionality of laws. The Second, Third, and Fourth Departments, known collectively as the "Evaluation Departments," share equal responsibility with each other and are responsible for evaluating Cabinet orders and proposed laws that originate in particular from the agencies. Their jurisdictions are organized as follows: the Second Department is in charge of proposals issued by the Cabinet, a part of the Prime Minister's Office, and the Ministry of Justice; the Third Department scrutinizes bills from the Ministry of Foreign Affairs, the Ministry of Finance, and the Ministry of Home Affairs; and the Fourth Department is responsible for MITI, the Ministry of Agriculture, Forestry, and Fisheries, and the Ministry of Transport. The bureau's Administration Office corresponds to the secretariat office of other agencies, and its status is lower than that of the four departments.

The Cabinet Legislation Bureau has the same number of employees as each Legislative Bureau in the houses of the Diet. The major difference between them is that high positions in the latter are filled by specially hired employees, while all high-level officials at the Cabinet Legislation Bureau have been recruited on temporary assignment from other agencies. Under each Cabinet Legislation Bureau department head are twenty-four counsellors in charge of interpreting and evaluating laws. After five years of service, they return to their original agencies. The current counsellors came there after having served as section chiefs at other agencies. Bureaucrats consider it a great honor to be appointed as counsellors of the Cabinet Legislation Bureau. Many former bureau counsellors have gone on to become administrative vice-ministers after returning to their own agencies; examples include such prominent officials as Chief Public Prosecutor Maeda Hiroshi, National Police Agency Director-General Yamada Hideo, Vice Foreign Minister and former Ambassador to the Soviet Union Takashima Masuo, Vice Finance Minister Sumita Satoshi, MITI Vice Minister Sugiyama Hiroshi, Vice Agriculture Minister

Nishimura Kenjiro, and Vice Construction Minister Awaya Toshinobu.

This illustrious list indicates that agencies have sent their best people to the Cabinet Legislation Bureau. Each counsellor of the bureau is responsible for evaluating proposed laws submitted by his own home agency; therefore if an agency sends an inept official to the bureau, the evaluation of its orders may be jeopardized. It is no wonder that the Ministry of Finance and the National Police Agency tend to send officials who have passed the National Bar Exam as undergraduates, a test of brilliancy, considering that fewer than ten undergraduates pass the exam each year. Of the twenty-four counsellors serving at the bureau at the time of writing, one-third had passed the National Bar Exam. After serving their five years, it would be possible for these counsellors to become lawyers without going through an apprenticeship at the National Legal Training and Research Institute like everyone else. The Cabinet Legislation Bureau is an elite organ; in Kasumigaseki an organization holds more power by being held in awe and relegated elite status than by having real leverage.

For an agency staffed by officials gathered from disparate agencies, the Cabinet Legislation Bureau is considered a united organization. As of the time of writing, officials at the bureau from other agencies with the rank of counsellor or higher included: four each from MITI, the Ministry of Finance and the Ministry of Justice; three from the Ministry of Home Affairs; two each from the Ministry of Agriculture, Forestry, and Fisheries, the Ministry of Health and Welfare, the Ministry of Foreign Affairs, and the Ministry of Transport; one each from the National Police Agency, the Ministry of Construction, the Ministry of Posts and Telecommunications, and the Ministry of Labor. The Cabinet Legislation Bureau is jointly run by MITI, the Ministry of Finance, the Ministry of Justice and the Ministry of Home Affairs, and these four ministries take turns in filling the highest post of director-general of the bureau. Surprisingly, there are no confrontations among the four with regard to personnel assignments. One reason is that appointments at the bureau to the rank of department head and above are handled very cautiously. Since counsellors return to their home agencies in five years, bureau chiefs are, as a rule, selected from among former counsellors of the Cabinet Legislation Bureau who have since returned to their home agencies. A new department head of the Cabinet Legislation Bureau will be briefed on whether he is destined for the more elite path that leads up to head of the First Department, then deputy director-general, and finally director-general of the Cabinet Legislation Bureau, or whether he will instead end up retiring at the rank of head of the Second Department or lower. No bureaucrat outside this tracking has ever been allowed to serve as top officials in the bureau. Consequently, no prime minister or LDP politician, regardless of political influence, has been able to interfere with the appointment of high officials in the bureau. The Cabinet Legislation Bureau has been considered the bureaucrat's "last stronghold" not only by resisting political manipulation, but through its autonomy in personnel management.

Tarnished by the Persian Gulf War. The Cabinet Legislation Bureau's elite image was battered by its handling of the proposal to deploy Self-Defense Forces aircraft during the Persian Gulf War. At issue was a change in the bureau's interpretation of the Self-Defense Forces Act. In late 1990, when confronted with a bill on cooperating with the United Nations peacekeeping operations (the PKO Bill), the Cabinet Legislation Bureau had stuck with its original position, which, in the words of a counsellor serving at the time was to "interpret the Act as narrowly as possible." When it came to the proposal to deploy Self-Defense Forces aircraft to the Persian Gulf region, however, the bureau switched to a broad, "activist" interpretation of the law. Even many bureau counsellors were astounded by the abrupt shift. Though the top officials at the Cabinet Legislation Bureau had repeatedly discussed the interpretation of the law and reportedly disagreed over many points, in the end, Director-General Kudo Atsuo prevailed. A special Cabinet order, pursuant to certain special provisions of the Self Defense Forces Act, allowed the Self-Defense Forces to send aircraft to the Persian Gulf region.

Was it that Director-General Kudo believed that as long as the deployment of aircraft did not constitute the use of force, it did not violate Article 9 of the Constitution, and thereby the bureau's narrow interpretation of the Constitution would not be compromised? Whatever the rationale, it is inadequate to explain the policy reversal from the interpretation in regard to the PKO bill a mere seven months earlier. Nor does it appear that Kudo gave in to the numerous LDP politicians who had been rashly calling for a political instead of bureaucratic appointment of the Cabinet Legislation Bureau director-general or even for a dissolution of the Cabinet Legislation Bureau. Nevertheless, undeniably political considerations colored Kudo's decision.

According to former Cabinet Legislation Bureau Director-General Takatsuji Masami, who was later appointed Supreme Court Justice: "The mission of the Cabinet Legislation Bureau is to ensure the Cabinet can proceed through legal means. The bureau should make its legal judgments based on what it believes to be right, strictly from a legal perspective; it should not take an irresponsible stand based on the government's political whims. The Cabinet trusts and respects the bureau's authority only when the bureau is true to its own principles."

In other words, bureaucrats and judges respect the bureau's authority because it has distanced itself from political considerations. It is no wonder, then, that a number of former Cabinet Legislation Bureau counsellors and top agency officials expressed the opinion that Kudo should have upheld his bureau's principles, even if at the price of his resignation. While if he had resigned a collapse of the administration would have been inevitable, that would have been a worthwhile price for maintaining the bureau's integrity. This viewpoint, perhaps, reflects the wishful thinking of bureaucrats who want to preserve the "last stronghold" of the bureaucracy.

After the Self-Defense Forces incident, the bureau has kept retreating from the forefront. Eventually, on the question of the PKO bill, it allowed the government to send Self-Defense Forces troops abroad. The Cabinet Legislation Bureau seems headed in the same irreversible direction as the Bank of Japan after its mistake in 1973 of succumbing to political influence and its subsequent loss of status and credibility.

The Ministry of Finance: A Vast Power Network

"The Communist Party elites of the former Soviet Union are now gone, but as far as I see from the practice of *amakudari*, the bureaucrats are the Japanese counterpart to the *nomenklatura* [privileged Soviet Communist party elites]" says Arai Hiroshi, a former top official of the National Police Agency. "The Ministry of Finance bureaucrats are a classic example. They have made sure to send at least one of their retired officials through *amakudari* to each public corporation and government agency-created organization. And on top of that, the Ministry of Finance also sends it currently active bureaucrats on temporary assignment to hold important posts in the relatively new agencies founded after World War II. There is no question that the Ministry of Finance has become extremely powerful since the demise of the Home Ministry in 1947. It is time to evaluate the ministry's methods, to consider whether they are legitimate, illegal, or harmful, and to determine why the ministry acquires such vast power."

The hard truth is that in all of Kasumigaseki, the Ministry of Finance consistently obtains the best *amakudari* positions for its retirees; it has connections everywhere, not only in the finance, insurance, and securities industries, as one would expect, but also in government financial organizations and public corporations. And it isn't only *amakudari*. Currently active finance officials on temporary assignment even serve in high-ranking posts of the Economic Planning Agency, the Defense Agency, the Environment Agency, the National Land Agency, and the Hokkaido Development Agency. This phenomenon has been termed "Ministry of Finance Control," but as Arai indicates, it is unclear why the ministry exercises as much influence as it does. Indeed, just how does the Ministry of Finance generate and maintain its web of power?

Claiming New Turf. Every December, the Ministry of Finance and MITI engage in a fierce debate over the "Government Economic Forecast for the Coming Year" that is issued by the Economic Planning Agency. While the Ministry of Finance aims to keep the expected GNP growth rate as low as possible, MITI wants to push it as high as possible. The Ministry of Finance prefers a low rate because it fears that a high rate will expand the budget, and the agencies will clamor for more money. MITI, on the other hand, wants a budget surplus for the years when the actual growth rate falls short of the projected rate. By pushing for a high projected growth rate, MITI makes it possible to request supplemental funds more easily.

It is commonly, but wrongly, assumed that the growth rate forecast is created from the Economic Planning Agency's econometric models. It is true that the agency independently calculates forecasts; however, these are not the figures that are released to the public. Actually, figures revealed to the public in the Government Economic Forecast are a compromise between the Ministry of Finance and MITI figures.

The two ministries also fight over the development process of the White Paper on the Economy, a collection of detailed economic analyses also published by the Economic Planning Agency. Both ministries scrutinize the smallest details to make sure that their respective self-interests are not compromised. They especially fear that the content of the White Paper on the Economy will contradict their forecasts, public image, and policy decisions. Although both ministries have strong influence over the government, neither can issue its own version of the Government Economic Forecast, or the White Paper on the Economy, under its own name. The Economic Planning Agency, as the Cabinet-level advisory agency in charge, serves as an intermediary between the two ministries and decides what figures should be released to the public. Because the two ministries know that extending their influence over this agency would strengthen their leverage in the making of government economic policy, each have fought viciously over assigning their economic experts to top posts there.

The Economic Planning Agency used to be called MITI's "crown land" (a reference to territory governed directly by a royal family) because MITI had a history of monopolizing this agency's important positions, including that of administrative vice-minister. MITI's stronghold at the planning agency had been established by officials from its prewar predecessor, the Ministry of Commerce and Industry, who had formed the nucleus of the agency's forerunner, the Economic Stability Bureau. Now, however, primary control of the Economic Planning

Agency rests with the Ministry of Finance, whose officials hold the top two posts. On this turn of events, a MITI official commented: "The Ministry of Finance outsmarted us. At MITI, we were preoccupied with personnel appointment in our own ministry, and generally did not send first-rate people to the planning agency. On the other hand, the Ministry of Finance sent some of their best people, and they were still on the fast track after returning to the Ministry of Finance." Indeed, service as director-general of the secretariat at the Economic Planning Agency has almost become a prerequisite for becoming administrative vice-minister at the Ministry of Finance.

The Ministry of Finance's strategy of sending high-caliber officials has worked. The Economic Planning Agency cannot afford to antagonize a future administrative vice-minister of the Ministry of Finance; thus, in deference to the Ministry of Finance, the agency lends a receptive ear to whoever is the director-general of the secretariat. Through this manner of exercising influence, the finance officials have taken the lead in the making of government economic policy.

The ministry adopted an entirely different strategy when it came to assigning its finance officials to positions of importance in the Defense Agency. The Defense Agency had been to the National Police Agency what the Economic Planning Agency formerly was to MITI, i.e., a "crown land." Police officials who had worked for the former Home Ministry had constituted the bulk of leadership in the National Police Reserve, the forerunner of the Self-Defense Forces. The result was that Police officials had been appointed in an unbroken succession to important posts at the Defense Agency, just as MITI officials had at the Economic Agency. In this case, the Ministry of Finance did not take a frontal approach by sending first-rate officials. Instead, they began quietly by sending Budget Bureau officials and chief examiners who had worked in defense budget making until it had succeeded in capturing the top posts. A former police official recalls: "The National Police Agency had it coming. We did not send officials to the Defense Agency according to calculated plans; rather, we sent them whenever it was convenient for us. Some officials returned immediately after we had sent them. Or we sent officials that we did not want to the Defense Agency. We dug our own grave."

Whereas Ministry of Finance officials were once limited to positions in the Defense Agency such as chief of the Accounting Division, they now seize top Defense Agency posts. The ministry has dominated, until recently, the post of administrative vice-minister throughout several administrations.

What motivated the Ministry of Finance to infiltrate the Defense Agency? Simply put, the ministry wanted to expand its colonies, that is, its territory, as much as it possibly could. But while the National Police Agency had been motivated to acquire Defense Agency positions to increase production of the colony's "local crop," that is, the military, the Ministry of Finance sought to control the growth of the crop. They understood that the crop, if given the proper conditions, could multiply extremely fast and that eventually the colony could eat up the treasury of the "home country," that is, the Ministry of Finance. To monitor the agency, the finance officials had sent in caretakers.

The Ministry of Finance gained control of both the Economic Planning Agency and the Defense Agency by skillfully deploying personnel and by brandishing power through the Budget Bureau. As its territories were further expanded through a process of "divide and conquer," the Ministry of Finance acquired a level of power never before obtained by other agencies. In the process, it helped to promote the self-interested competitiveness that permeates the bureaucracy. Agencies now fight over seemingly trivial matters to enhance their self-interest and expand their turf. For example, conflicts persist between the Ministry of Justice and the National Police Agency; the Ministry of Foreign Affairs and MITI; the Ministry of Construction and the Ministry of Home Affairs; MITI and the Ministry of Posts and Telecommunications; the Ministry of Construction and the Ministry of Agriculture, Forestry, and Fisheries, and so on. One official at the Ministry of Finance's Budget Bureau offers this defense: "Vertical administration and interagency power struggles have a positive side. Power struggles invigorate the government as a whole by encouraging the agencies to come up with new ideas, and keeping the government's self-renewal process going." However, this attitude disguises the fact that the Ministry of Finance actually enjoys seeing other agencies fight each other and waste energy. When such battles are at a stalemate, the ministry will step in as an intermediary, and the more interagency battles break out, the more chances for the ministry to act as a go-between and increase its leverage. By keeping the agencies from uniting in an anti-Ministry of Finance front, the Ministry of Finance further secures its interests, and their power keeps growing and broadening.

Sources of Power.   In scrutinizing the origins of the Ministry of Finance's power and influence, we need to assess the legitimacy of the agency's ability to colonize agencies or mediate amongst them. The Ministry of Finance's first and foremost power is the right of its Budget Bureau to formulate the budget. Every December, officials of all agencies rent vast numbers of futons and prepare to stay overnight in the office for the budget-making period. This must be the most ridiculous spectacle among Kasumigaseki's many annual rituals. But every responsible official must go through with this because the Budget Bureau may telephone at any time, even in the middle of the night. Officials must remain ready for any question.

The following is a typical scenario. The Budget Bureau calls an agency in the middle of the night and asks a division chief to report to the Budget Bureau. The division chief rushes to the Budget Bureau accompanied by a subordinate who carries resource materials. At the Budget Bureau, a chief examiner, a rank equivalent to assistant section chief in other agencies, is in charge of negotiations. A budget examiner, (the position directly above a chief examiner), regularly works with agency councillors and bureau chiefs who rank at least two stages above him. Throughout this process, bureaucrats from other agencies gradually come under the impression that finance bureaucrats are in a class by themselves.

The late night budget-making activity produces a strange phenomenon that can be compared to a psychological condition in which people who are being held as hostages or are confined in a hijacked aircraft begin to strongly identify with their captors. This syndrome became evident during the 1970 hijack of a Japan Air Lines flight by Japanese Red Army members. When the plane landed in Pyongyang,

North Korea, the passengers were reportedly in tears on parting from their hijackers, and some were even said to have joined in an impromptu rendition of a "revolutionary song" in sympathy with their perpetrators.

In a similar manner, friendships often develop between the Ministry of Finance bureaucrats and the officials at other agencies. A camaraderie emerges in the closed environment in which budget negotiations last well into the night or early morning. In principle the bureaucrats from other agencies are supposed to be critical of the way the budget is made, but at some point during the arduous process they gradually develop sympathy toward the Ministry of Finance officials and are "sold." More often than not, the friendships formed during the budget-making process last a lifetime. The ministry not only keeps other agencies in check through its Budget Bureau, but also brings officials from other agencies to its side through the budget-making process. This is a fact relatively unknown to most people outside the system.

The Ministry of Finance's ability to control Kasumigaseki involves more than just a strong Budget Bureau. They also have several other weapons that they skillfully deploy. For example, when the New Land Tax Law became an issue in the media, it was publicized as an attempt to contain exceedingly high land prices by reducing real estate prices. But this was not the Ministry of Finance's true motive in drafting this law. Rather, it was an attempt to force the Ministry of Home Affairs to assume the burden of responsibility for reducing local allocation tax grants, an item that constitutes about one-third of the national budget. The Budget Bureau has the power to cut the budgets of government agencies, but local allocation tax grants, which are under the jurisdiction of the Ministry of Home Affairs, account for a fixed percentage of tax revenues by law and they are off limits to the bureau. To get its way, finance officials widely publicized the idea that Japan was a country with "a poor national government and rich local governments," and threatened to impose a land tax if the supposedly wealthy localities failed to charge a sufficient property tax instead of continuing to rely heavily on local allocation tax grants. If this were done, the Ministry of Finance's tax revenues would increase, and it would then be in a position to put pressure on the Ministry of Home Affairs to change grant distribution under the law.

In any case, the Ministry of Finance's deadly weapons, that is, its power through the Tax Bureau to set tax rates and determine what are taxable items, should never be underestimated. The Ministry of Finance's National Tax Administration Agency, the Japanese counterpart of the U.S. Internal Revenue Service, can apply pressure upon other agencies through the industries that fall into their jurisdictions, by strictly enforcing tax collection. The ability to tax is a great source of its power. Another significant contributor to the Ministry of Finance's power base is the Financial Bureau. This bureau controls the Fiscal Investment and Loan Program (FILP), in essence the second-largest budget in the nation and five percent of the national budget in 1992. While the Budget Bureau addresses the budgets of the agencies, the Financial Bureau handles the budgets of public corporations. The Budget Bureau, Tax Bureau, and Financial Bureau constitute the foundation of the Ministry of Finance's power.

The Ministry of Finance possesses further weapons, namely, the ability to appoint secretaries to the Prime Minister's Office and to the Chief Cabinet Secretary. The secretaries appointed to these Cabinet and Cabinet Secretariat offices are career bureaucrats from MITI, the Ministry of Finance, the Ministry of Foreign Affairs, and the National Police Agency. But the Ministry of Foreign Affairs and the National Police Agency are expected to send secretaries to these offices because of their agencies' jurisdictions, while the Ministry of Finance sends a secretary to both the Prime Minister's Office and the Chief Cabinet Secretary for no explicit reason. Not just any agency sends secretaries to these destinations: MITI acquired a secretary to the prime minister spot only in recent years, and the Ministry of Home Affairs has been lobbying for a secretary spot of its own by emphasizing the importance of domestic policy, but has been unsuccessful. The main reason for this failure is that, with the exception of foreign policy and police, the top ten policy fields have been dominated by the Ministry of Finance, which refuses to create room for other agencies to participate.

That is not all. The Ministry of Finance dominates important positions in the Prime Minister's Office, including head of the

Councillors' Office on Internal Affairs, and the Labor and Public Corporations Office. The Ministry of Finance is able to monitor every move of the prime minister's inner circle, and even supervises the flow of information from agencies to the prime minister. The Ministry of Finance also practically controls the Board of Audit, the Japanese counterpart of the U.S. General Accounting Office. The Ministry of Finance has claimed one out of every three inspector positions, head of the First Bureau, and important posts in the Fifth Bureau. Bureaucrats hate the Board of Audit's intense scrutiny; almost all agencies feel strangled when the board watches over not only budget allocation but also how that money is spent.

The Fair Trade Commission (FTC) is another tool that the Ministry of Finance manipulates to control other agencies. The Ministry of Finance has retained the post of FTC chairman for ten years and also has filled other important posts in the FTC's Secretariat. Not only is the Ministry of Finance able to control other agencies in terms of budgeting. It also has the resources to meddle with their internal administrative practices by using the FTC to criticize the way economic agencies such as MITI and the Ministry of Transport have conducted "administrative guidance."

The Ministry of Finance is also able to interfere with personnel management in other agencies by filling the post of chief of the Second Compensation Division in the Bureau of Compensation of the National Personnel Authority who manages the levels of all government employees' salaries depending on their rank and the number of employees at each ranking. Consequently, if an agency wants to raise the average wage for its employees, it has to consult this division chief. The division chief then might ask the agency to lower some employees' pay to compensate for raising the pay of others; he would not want agencies to be too generous to their employees and thereby increase government spending. If, on the other hand, an agency wanted to create a new position rather than raising pay, it must consult the director-general of the Administrative Management Bureau at the Management and Coordination Agency, yet another position filled by a finance bureaucrat. The Administrative Management Bureau is in charge of agencies' organization, quotas for personnel, and director posts; it generally refuses to allow individual agencies to change their own structure or increase director posts.

On every important topic in the bureaucracy—funding, information, personnel, and even administrative practices—the Ministry of Finance has a say in other agencies' business. Widely known as "the agency that tops other agencies" and "a bureaucracy within the bureaucracy," the Ministry of Finance presides over a process in which control begets greater control. But just how long can its dominating power last? The major agencies are deeply resentful of the Ministry of Finance's vast power network. In some cases, agencies have successfully seized on an issue, brought the Diet and public opinion to their side and defeated the Ministry of Finance's schemes. But these are exceptions. Agencies are usually powerless in attempting to overthrow the Ministry of Finance's iron hand.

Nevertheless, the ministry's dominant rule finally seems to be heading past its prime. The turning point came with the disclosure of scandals in the financial and securities industries upon the "bursting" of the so-called bubble economy of the 1980s. The Ministry of Finance has maintained that it and its bureaucrats have, on the whole, conducted relatively trouble-free public administrations, and it has continued its practice of seizing high positions in other agencies. But the succession of scandals in the financial and securities industries has demonstrated that its claims of innocence could not be further from the truth. Many bureaucrats now say that the myth of an invincible Ministry of Finance has been debunked. The agencies are poised to put the tarnished Ministry of Finance on the defensive.

MITI: The Rise of the "Industry Regulation" Faction

Many agencies in Kasumigaseki are faced with radical changes in their jurisdictions. Unable to break with their traditional standard operating procedures or change their established structure, such agencies have shown on many occasions that they cannot cope with present-day needs or unanticipated problems. However, MITI is one agency that would have lost its reason for existing if it had continued with business as usual. The industries that fall under its supervision have developed so dramatically that they can no longer be reigned in. Too proud to let themselves become second-rate, MITI officials have responded by rebuilding their agency into the "think tank of Kasumigaseki." Today, MITI is again at a crossroads: it must continue to redefine its role and at the same time avoid the divisive internal policy disputes that occasionally arise among its officials. In order to understand how MITI policies are decided and to anticipate the nature of future policy decisions, it would be useful to examine how MITI bureaucrats reacted to the U.S.–Japan summit meeting of January 1992.

Amidst U.S.–Japan Trade Friction.   The January 1992 U.S.–Japan summit meeting was, more than anything else, an "auto summit." The main agenda addressed how many U.S. automobiles and automotive parts the Japanese automobile industry would be expected buy. The "Tokyo declaration," issued jointly by President Bush and Prime Minister Miyazawa, included a clause on a purchasing "action plan" which mentioned numerical targets for the Japanese automobile industry on the purchase of U.S. autos and auto parts. In particular, the "action plan" stated that five Japanese auto makers were ready to import 1,200 to 6,000 cars each from the Big Three, an unusual measure considering the context of the entire history of U.S.–Japan trade disputes. These targets were obviously contradictory to other sections of the declaration, which emphasized both nations' commitment to the principle of free trade. Even some high officials at MITI, which had been in charge of negotiating the deal with the automobile industry, considered the numerical targets abnormal.

Kumano Hideaki, who, when interviewed, was director-general of MITI's Machinery and Information Industries Bureau, made the following comment about his negotiations with the automobile industry: "MITI did not ask the auto makers to accept the purchase quotas. Rather, we emphasized the need to cooperate with the U.S. We explained to them that since Japan was part of the global community, it is particularly important to maintain good relations with the U.S." Kawashima Atsushi, who was then chief of the Automobile Division at the Machinery and Information Industries Bureau, explained: "MITI and the automobile industry exchanged opinions and information. MITI told the auto industry exactly what the White House and the U.S. automobile industry wanted." Kawashima emphasized that the decision to include quotas in the declaration had been made voluntarily by the Japanese auto industry.

While it is true that Japan operates as a market economy and that MITI has no authority to force companies to import finished goods, either by law or administrative guidance, it is also true that behind the negotiations between the Machinery and Information Industries Bureau and the automobile industry had stood MITI's firm "resolve." In his talks with the auto industry leaders, Tanahashi Yuji, former administrative vice-minister of MITI, argued: "Since the end of World War II, Japan had been able to come this far and to gain individual liberties due to the generous assistance of the U.S. What would have happened to us had the Soviet Union occupied Japan? We should be grateful to the U.S." Thus it was that in preparation for President Bush's visit to Japan, Tanahashi had recommended that Japanese businesses put national gratitude towards the U.S. into action. MITI had negotiated with the Japanese automobile industry to insure the success of the January 1992 summit meeting.

On this issue, MITI's method of dealing with the automobile industry has provoked criticism not just from the industry itself but other leading industries. They have expressed concern that MITI might be heading in the direction of advocating full-scale managed trade. In all trade disputes between Japan and outside countries, including past disputes in industries such as textiles, steel, batteries, sewing machines, automobiles, cameras, television sets, VCRs, and semiconductors, MITI had called for both voluntary export restraints and import share targets. Now, however, the industries feared that MITI's demands may go one step further, as it had done in the present negotiations over imports of U.S. automobiles.

On the other hand, MITI fears that if Japan's internationally competitive industries such as automobiles, consumer electronics, and semiconductors continue to grow at present rates, not only will they cause further trade disputes but they will also create problems in domestic industrial production. Every time there has been a trade dispute, MITI officials have debated whether or not to ask industries for "voluntary restraint," with the idea of taking measures in the form of policy making if that does not work. Some officials have stated, "We did not become MITI officials to clean up after companies such as Toyota and NEC that contribute to trade disputes because they are over-competitive." Ironically, as private companies become more and more independent they do not want to listen to MITI. MITI is now being dragged around in the mud by the very industries it has done so much to promote.

Three Factions at MITI.   How did the bureaucrats "clean up the auto-mobile industry's act," even as they struggled to finish preparations for President Bush's visit to Japan? And how did they succeed despite an internal split into three camps of opinion over agency policy? In late February 1992, in an effort to clarify the split in MITI, I inter-viewed twenty MITI bureaucrats. Eight of these were high officials (including bureau chiefs, and deputy director-generals, and a director-general of the secretariat), and twelve section chiefs or the equivalent. I found that basically MITI breaks down into three ideological fac-tions:

1. *The laissez faire faction.* MITI should leave industries alone and intervene only when a trade dispute occurs. Thirty percent of the interviewees belonged to this faction.
2. *The industry-regulation faction.* The competitiveness of Japanese companies is self-destructive. MITI must not only regulate trade but also strengthen domestic industri-al policy. Twenty percent of the interviewees belonged to this faction.
3. *The middle-of-the-road faction, or industry-guidance faction.* Even though there are problems with Japanese business "ethics," MITI should guide rather than regulate compa-nies to resolve trade disputes. Fifty percent of the intervie-wees belonged to this faction.

According to MITI insiders, these three divisions can be said to reflect the major political views of the entire agency. A retired high-ranking official creates the following picture of the present leadership of MITI:

> Administrative Vice-Minister Tanahashi has pro-regulation tendencies. Sakamoto Yoshihiro, former director-general of the Basic Industries Bureau and who is now vice-minister for International Affairs, is a strong pro-regulation advocate. Naito Masahisa, former director-general of the secretariat, is in the laissez faire faction. The views of others, such as Kumano Hideaki, former chief of the Machinery and Information Industries Bureau and Yamamoto Kosuke, former chief of the Industrial Policy Bureau [who is now, through *amakudari*, an executive at Toyota], lie somewhere in between Sakamoto and Naito.

Let us now take a closer look at the views held by members of each of these three factions within MITI according to comments from of each of the officials mentioned above.

Naito Masahisa, a leading laissez faire advocate though he now has retired from the bureaucracy, has stated:

> Both government and private enterprise have furthered the cause of internationalization, but the gap that lies between them has not been bridged. Business corporations tend to lose discipline because they don't really understand anything outside of how the economy works. I think that as Japanese companies encounter friction overseas and make mistakes, they will learn from this experience and improve themselves. MITI should maintain a long-term perspective and deal with problems whenever necessary. The only way to address problems is by persuasion. It's okay if there are mavericks among the companies, because those mavericks might change, just as Matsushita Electronic Corporation [Panasonic] developed from an isolated domestic company into a global concern.

Laissez faire advocates condemn those bureaucrats arrogant enough to believe that they alone have principle and discipline in contrast to the depravity of private enterprise. They are loathe to kill the creative potential of private companies and seem to tolerate problems that result from efforts to "sell good products at affordable prices."

The industry regulation faction holds views opposite to the laissez faire faction. Sakamoto Yoshihiro, a proponent of this position, states:

> Society as a whole, not just business, has become increasingly money-oriented. It is a time for soul-searching for us all, including bureaucrats. The executives of the companies that cause problems are not necessarily bad people, but technocrats have taken over. Concepts such as fairness, compassion, and coexistence have been set aside, and trade disputes have increased. Failure to establish firm civilian control over the military led to Japan's defeat in World War II. If we leave the technocrats to continue as they please, we may repeat the same results. Business people must be made to learn that in a society and a nation there are things that are more important than monetary profit.

Sakamoto's remark echoes a remark by the late Amaya Naohiro, former vice-minister of MITI, made more than ten years ago during a trade dispute on the automobile industry. Amaya had said: "The Japanese automobile industry acts like the Imperial Japanese Army and Navy," a reference to Japan's failure to contain the growth of its armed forces in the 1930s, which eventually led to the war in China and the Pacific.

The movement to regulate industry has been on the rise in MITI for the last several years. A report issued by MITI in 1987 entitled "The Future of the Machinery and Information Industries" states: "Individual companies should stop launching a constant flood of exports and begin to make their export, production and investment plans according to long term prospects of global markets. If this fails to work, the government should regulate exports by trade control and other measures in order to prevent overproduction and excessive investment in production facilities." At the time, the guidelines proposed in this report never materialized. This was because of "MITI's inadequacy," according to a section chief at the Machinery and Information Industries Bureau. But these ideas have again resurfaced during the most recent trade dispute over automobiles.

According to a section chef at the Industrial Policy Bureau, the industry-regulation faction is interested in influencing MITI into enacting, either through legal means or the practice of administrative guidance, the following measures:

1. Identify what portion of business-related activities such as transportation, environment, safety, and general costs of maintaining an overseas presence, should be covered by businesses, and require them to pay their fair share.
2. Consolidate industries, such as the automobile industry, by mergers.
3. Legalize holding companies and strengthen corporate control over companies.
4. Increase prosecution of companies that engage in illegal practices contrary to fair competition such as dumping exports abroad and underpricing at home.
5. Reform the tax code for company stocks to prevent companies from excessively pursuing profits.

The third faction, the middle-of-the-road or industry-guidance faction appears to claim more than 50 percent, in other words the majority, of all MITI bureaucrats. Yamamoto Kosuke, an advocate of this faction, states: "Capitalism certainly is all about freedom. But just as Max Weber said, capitalism cannot function without 'discipline' and 'ethics.' These ideas are common sense in Western nations." Almost all officials in the industry guidance faction commonly bring up the word "ethics." Yamamoto continues: "MITI has 'guided' and 'set directions' for businesses according to its vision, and has, most of the time, been on the right track. MITI still directs high technology development and structural adjustments in the same manner. We can continue on this path; however, we must quickly adjust the gap between Japan and foreign countries in such areas as the number of hours in the work week. If we decrease work hours, then even the automobile industry would become less competitive."

A section chief at the Industrial Policy Bureau elaborates on Yamamoto's remark: "We think that certain industries, such as automobiles, consumer electronics, and semiconductors are lacking in 'ethics.' By adopting the standards and rules of other countries, we can control the behavior of companies that want to 'sell good products at affordable prices.'" Another section chief stated: "Japanese industries are becoming increasingly competitive. The only way we will resolve trade disputes is to raise the price of goods by increasing the cost of production."

The industry-guidance faction sounds moderate in its suggested measures, but its attitude seems as distrustful of companies as the industry-regulation faction. Perhaps for that reason, many of the officials in the industry-guidance faction welcomed the essay entitled "Japanese-Style Management in Danger" that was published in February 1992 by Morita Akio, chairman of Sony corporation. Prior to its publication, the essay had been distributed among top MITI officials. On January 28, Morita gave a lecture to the "Study Group on New Corporate Identity" of the Industrial Policy Bureau's Business Behavior Division, stating: "I started a company with forty-five people. Now the company employs more than forty thousand people, 60 percent of whom are non-Japanese. As for myself, I think there are limits to Japanese-style management." In the essay, Morita argued that the world is increasingly intolerant of Japanese companies' slogan about "selling good products at affordable prices," and Japan needs to institute such corrective measures as shorter working hours, increased pay, matching of Western shareholding procedures, equalizing of *keiretsu* companies, increasing contributions to a global society, protecting the environment, and saving energy and natural resources. (The term *keiretsu* refers to large Japanese business groups in which a single company owns companies in different industries.)

A majority of MITI bureaucrats were highly critical of Morita's essay, exclaiming: "When Japan and the EC disputed over VCRs, it was Mr. Morita who said, 'We make no apologies for selling good products at affordable prices.' Having co-authored *The Japan That Can Say No*, what right does Mr. Morita have in saying that now? Why then doesn't Sony begin practicing what Mr. Morita preaches?" However, despite a barrage of such criticism, many members of the industry guidance faction actually welcomed Morita's bold essay because it expressed views very similar to their own agenda to "adopt foreign standards to correct Japanese practices."

Indeed, the Industrial Policy Bureau is an instrumental government force behind the national effort to reduce work hours in Japan. "We are going to create a consortium in each industry and make it easier for companies to institute shorter working hours," said an enthusiastic Yamamoto. "We will cooperate with the Ministry of Labor to accomplish this goal, and, if it is necessary, we will ask for authorization from the FTC. We are also drafting laws that would protect small and medium-size enterprises and suppliers that might be affected by such changes." MITI's hope for successfully reducing work hours is surprisingly high. Some officials remarked, "Shorter hours may encourage companies to be more efficient, making them more, not less competitive." However, 70 percent of the twenty bureaucrats interviewed stated the real intent of the measure: "Reduced hours will definitely be effective in keeping the overly competitive industries, such as automobiles, in check." For example, Kumano offered this highly optimistic prediction: "The automobile markets are quickly approaching a saturation point. In other industries, too, small businesses are already defecting from the *keiretsu* system and refusing to supply large companies. Moreover, we are suffering from a labor shortage. Japan will have to adapt to these changes and companies will be forced to redefine their roles." Former Vice-Minister for General Affairs Watanabe Osamu, who is now head of the Machinery and Information Industries Bureau, also stated: "Reduced work hours will be effective. To change corporate behavior, we should be more aggressive in establishing rules. If initial measures do not succeed in altering corporate behavior, we should turn to measures such as regulation."

What shape will future MITI policies take? While the industry guidance faction now maintains a majority at MITI, that situation may not last. If U.S.–Japan trade disputes get worse, and U.S. criticism of Japan becomes more severe, the industry regulation faction may gain influence and power. Or, if the current recession in Japan lingers, and its effect on industries becomes more desperate, the "flexible response" solution advocated by the industry guidance faction may prove to be insufficient. Yet another scenario may be that companies will change their behavior on their own initiative and begin to tell MITI to "mind its own business." MITI then would have nowhere to go. Since there are limits to what MITI's industrial policies can accomplish, it must be pragmatic in its response to changes in the Japanese economy in order to continue its own existence. In any event, the era in which MITI was notoriously powerful has now come to an end.

The Ministry of Foreign Affairs: An Object of Scorn

Everyone in Kasumigaseki loves to hate the Ministry of Foreign Affairs. Bureaucrats from the other agencies become hostile and irritated whenever matters related to the Ministry of Foreign Affairs arise. This is not only because the ministry interferes with the business of other agencies and that the agencies resent it; that variety of power struggle is actually quite common in Kasumigaseki. There are deeper reasons for their resentment.

Surprisingly, officials from other agencies who have worked as attachés at Japanese embassies and consulates are quite critical of the Ministry of Foreign Affairs. Since they were living and working far away from Kasumigaseki in a foreign environment, one would expect these attachés to return to Japan as friends of the ambassadors and embassy staff. However, almost all former attachés express hostility towards the ministry. A retired high official of an economic agency who worked at an embassy in a Middle Eastern country stated: "In public, foreign affairs officials say they are taking care of agency business. In fact, all these officials do is show up at various parties, collect gossip, and then pass this off as 'intelligence gathering.' At well-equipped embassies, they entertain dignitaries from Japan's political and business worlds as well." A coordinating agency official stationed at an embassy in North America stated, "Ministry of Foreign Affairs officials discriminate against attachés like us by keeping an exclusive social circle; for example, they would not let us play golf with them on holidays."

Attaché System Under Fire.   In June 1991, anti-Ministry of Foreign Affairs sentiment flared during the "world conference" of the Third Provisional Council for Administrative Reform. With a few exceptions, including Matsunaga Nobuo, the former administrative vice-minister, an overwhelming majority of the twenty-seven conference members criticized the Ministry of Foreign Affairs. Their suggestions included "establishing a minister-at-large for foreign policy," "appointing private citizens as ambassadors," and "abolishing the Diplomatic Service Examination." The Ministry of Foreign Affairs was taken aback.

To defuse the criticism, the Ministry of Foreign Affairs formed a group made up of important bureaucrats, including vice-ministers and counsellors, to defend its case. Led by Sato Yoshiyasu, then director-general of the secretariat, the group members lobbied the world conference members, patiently explained where the Ministry of Foreign Affairs stood, and then asked for their support. Seki Hiromoto, former chief of the South American Bureau, had many acquaintances among the conference members and was visiting them "at the request of the director-general of the secretariat." He told me: "I just don't agree with the argument that everything will go fine as soon as we abolish the Diplomatic Service Examination. What about other agencies that hire through the Entrance Examinations for the National Civil Service? They still are fighting the same old jurisdictional battles."

In the end, the conference conceded to the Ministry of Foreign Affairs and chose to ignore the proposed reform measures. The world conference members included not only former bureaucrats but members from the media, academia, labor unions, the business world, and agricultural cooperatives. How could such a diverse group of people agree, however temporarily, on their criticism of the Ministry of Foreign Affairs? A widely accepted explanation claims that agencies such as MITI, the Ministry of Finance, and the Ministry of Agriculture, Forestry, and Fisheries effectively persuaded the conference members, mostly those holding close ties to the named agencies, to turn against the Ministry of Foreign Affairs. Bureaucrats from the other major agencies apparently seized on the conference as a perfect opportunity to vent their anger towards the ministry.

Considering the current trend towards internationalization in many aspects of Japanese society, it has become essential that Japan's government agencies cooperate, under the leadership of the Ministry of Foreign Affairs, in formulating Japanese foreign policy. More than ever before, it is vital for the government's overseas establishments to use the attaché system effectively and to provide timely, accurate and detailed intelligence, i.e. information plus analysis, on foreign countries. However, the "Report on the Present State of Overseas Establishments," issued in June 1991 by the Administrative Inspection Bureau of the Management and Coordination Agency, describes the attaché system as follows:

> In 1990, there were 429 attachés, representing 17 percent of the total number of employees at overseas establishments. Their expertise was mostly in economic fields. The attaché system was designed to deploy officials with specialized knowledge and expertise from agencies other than the Ministry of Foreign Affairs so that the ministry does not have to train and maintain experts in all fields on its own. The system has become integral to our diplomatic network by strengthening the overseas establishments and improving the standards of Japanese diplomacy as a whole. On the other hand, overseas establishments, particularly those with a large number of attachés, experience problems with the system: depending on what attachés and their home agencies think of tours of duty at overseas establishments and what actual tasks the attachés perform, an *unevenness in staff workload has risen because tasks have become rigid and routine, and that may hinder a coherent policy on organizational management* [emphasis added]. Meanwhile, it is imperative that the attaché system perform better as our diplomacy expands in the midst of increasingly complex bilateral relationships, largely centered around economic issues and trends, toward a new, multilateral world order. We can envision an increased proximity between the Ministry of Foreign Affairs and other agencies in an effort to deal with these issues. It is hoped that the attaché system will improve.

Since this report was issued by a government agency under political and administrative constraints, many passages simply beat around the bush. The reality is much more serious than the report lets on. Former attachés agree that foreign affairs bureaucrats distance themselves from the attachés. Evidently, the power struggles at Kasumigaseki have only been transplanted to the closed foreign environment called overseas establishments, and they often take on an emotional character. It is for this reason that the attaché system essentially does not work. Most attachés return to Japan seething with resentment towards the foreign affairs bureaucrats at the helm of overseas establishments. Regardless of who is to blame for the mismanagement of the attaché system, it has produced many enemies for the Ministry of Foreign Affairs.

A Covetous Nature.   There is more to the attaché system than is first apparent. When an agency sends an attaché to the Ministry of Foreign Affairs, the latter sets the conditions for accepting that official, including requests for additional officials to look after the attaché in the foreign country, help him or her learn the local language, manage the office, and so on. This support staff of additional non-career officials is often referred to by the derogatory term *tenmasen*, or "barge." In other words, they are towed along behind the main ship (the attaché) like a supply barge.

The *tenmasen* system was introduced in 1975 when other agencies agreed to send "one additional official per attaché" to alleviate a personnel shortage at the Ministry of Foreign Affairs. Since then the ministry has been asking for more and more additional officials when new attachés are assigned to legations. The director-general of the secretariat at a coordinating ministry stated:

> If our agency attempts to send an attaché to a prominent place like Washington or Paris, the Ministry of Foreign Affairs will demand at least four, probably six *tenmasen* officials. Agencies such as the Ministry of Posts and Telecommunications or the Ministry of Agriculture, Forestry, and Fisheries have no problem with that because they have many officials to spare. But small agencies like ours simply don't have the numbers. This is the reason why we cannot ask the ministry to let us send more attachés to more destinations, although we would like to.

Here is another such comment from an agency official: "A few years ago, the Ministry of Posts and Telecommunications dispatched more than ten additional officials to accompany a new first secretary." And another: "When an agency elevates a first secretary to counsellor of a mission at an embassy in a first-rate nation, the ministry demands that more *tenmasen* officials be sent." And still another: "Even when the Ministry of Foreign Affairs itself asks for attachés, an agency must still send additional officials."

Each December, the ministry meets with representatives from the various agencies to negotiate over attachés. This occurs after all agencies agree with the Management and Coordination Agency on the numbers of attachés to send. Agencies who want to send new attachés give a list of proposed nations to the Ministry of Foreign Affairs, which then decides the number of *tenmasen* officials for each new attaché request and asks the agencies to supply them. According to a former secretariat section chief: "In many cases, three *tenmasen* officials per attaché were required for a first-rate destination, which includes industrialized nations such as the U.S. and Western European nations and two *tenmasen* per attaché for a second-rate destination. The Ministry of Foreign Affairs even said that if we sent a second secretary and additional officials to a third-rate nation, which we weren't even interested in, it would then approve our bid for a first-rate spot."

The *tenmasen* system has two main problems. As a result of greater demand from the Ministry of Foreign Affairs for *tenmasen* officials, the small agencies find it increasingly difficult to send new attachés, while large agencies are relatively unaffected. For example, agencies such as the Economic Planning Agency, the Science and Technology Agency, and the Environment Agency want to improve their intelligence network overseas, but most of the time they have to make do with what they have because they lack available *tenmasen* officials. Why then does the ministry make such preposterous demands upon the smaller agencies? A high official at the Ministry of Finance's Budget Bureau claims, "We are asking the Ministry of Foreign Affairs to use common sense." However, there are few signs that the ministry has heeded this advice. Foreign affairs officials should be more forthcoming on why up to more than ten additional officials are required to support the business of an attaché. The other government agencies have grown increasingly skeptical of the ministry's explanation that the extra staff is necessary to support their overseas establishments and have come to view the *tenmasen* system as being designed to discourage to dispatch of attachés.

Another problem with the *tenmasen* system is the treatment of these non-career officials who are sent overseas. Most *tenmasen* officials are assigned to legations in developing countries in Africa, Southeast Asia, the Middle East, and South America, regardless of where the attachés have been posted. *Tenmasen* officials are formally referred to as "important secretariat personnel," but in fact, they are assigned everyday, incidental administrative tasks. While attachés receive several months of training before their overseas assignment and are paid more than twice as much as they are in Japan, *tenmasen* officials get no special training and receive only small stipends in addition to their regular pay. When I asked a ranking member of a labor union in an economic agency about this disparity in treatment, he could not give a coherent explanation: "Is the position really called *tenmasen*? Our secretariat calls it 'personnel exchange with the Ministry of Foreign Affairs.' Come to think of it, when our agency sends non-career officials to overseas branches of public corporations, we carefully consider the appropriateness of the person for job. But in the case of sending people to embassies and consulates, it doesn't seem to matter who we choose to send."

When an agency searches its ranks for employees to serve in *tenmasen* posts, none are told that they are in effect "hostages" in exchange for an agency's opportunity to send attachés. In public, agencies say that they send only those who apply for these positions as additional officials. In actuality, many officials, typically non-career officials, receive *katatataki*, literally "a tap on the shoulder," and are forced to go on assignment. These people typically return to Japan before their term is out, mentally and physically exhausted.

A high official at the Ministry of Foreign Affairs has defended the practice in these words: "The agencies send attachés primarily to Western nations or other desirable regions. Consequently, the our officials would only be left to staff regions where climate and living conditions are so poor that no one wants to go there. I feel sorry for the *tenmasen* officials, but we have to maintain a sense of equality between the Ministry of Foreign Affairs and other agencies." While he may have a point as far as a sense of equality is concerned, this does not sufficiently explain why the Ministry of Foreign Affairs has greatly increased the number of *tenmasen* officials per attaché since the agreement of 1975 that specified one *tenmasen* official per attaché. Moreover, while foreign affairs officials make sure to have a support system if they themselves are to go to places where living conditions are difficult, *tenmasen* officials are denied this assistance.

The Ministry of Foreign Affairs would be well-advised to be more aware of the negative sentiments of other agencies, particularly in regard to the *tenmasen* system. Having already alienated former attachés in other ways, the ministry has few sympathizers, and the *tenmasen* system has fueled further mistrust. Before defending itself before the world conference members or demanding a greater role for itself, the Ministry of Foreign Affairs would be well advised to do research on why it is so despised in Kasumigaseki.

The Ministry of Construction: Infiltrated by Politicians

The agencies in the Japanese bureaucracy, ever sensitive to government power struggles, were always keeping a close eye on the infighting within the LDP's more powerful groups, such as the Takeshita faction led by Takeshita Noboru. The Ministry of Construction, long under the tight control of the "Kanemaru-Takeshita axis," had a vested interest in the Takeshita faction. In fact, the Ministry of Construction is infiltrated by the influence of *zoku* legislators connected to the construction industry, who are the most powerful such group of politicians in Japan.

Dominating Public Works Projects. One evening in early April of 1990, near the conclusion of the Structural Impediments Initiative (SII) talks between the U.S. and Japan, Kanemaru Shin, (at the time the strongest "shadow controller" in Japan and the leader of construction *zoku* legislators) stated: "Because of the SII talks, we will end up spending 400 trillion yen on social infrastructure in the next ten years." His remark quickly spread throughout the Diet, and construction *zoku* legislators welcomed it with enthusiasm. In the SII talks, the Americans had demanded that Japan introduce a multi-year plan for public works and social infrastructure at the cost of approximately ten percent of its GNP. The Ministry of Finance fiercely resisted specific numerical goals, but finally settled on a pledge to "invest 430 trillion yen on public works over ten years." This settlement was seen as a result of Kanemaru's political skill.

The Ministry of Construction, the Ministry of Transport, and the Ministry of Agriculture, Forestry, and Fisheries, nicknamed the "Three Dynasties," control more than 90 percent of public works projects in Japan. Of the Three Dynasties, the Ministry of Construction, which is in charge of roads, housing, and sewage, among other spheres, claims an overwhelming 68 percent. The Ministry of Agriculture, Forestry, and Fisheries, whose jurisdiction includes fishing ports, claims approximately 20 percent. The Ministry of Transport's jurisdiction encompasses seaports and airports, and it claims about six percent of public works projects.

Among LDP *zoku* legislators, the Three Dynasties would be those legislators connected with the three areas of agriculture, construction and commerce, but here too, construction *zoku* legislators dominate. For LDP politicians, the Ministry of Construction has been a rich source of votes and money. The construction industry as well is a dependable source of money because it lobbies politicians to win lucrative public works projects. There are 500,000 construction companies in Japan. With 40 percent of the total public investment in construction coming in the form of public works, if a public works project is particularly large, construction companies will do anything to win it. As a consequence, their huge financial contributions to politicians have become a fixture in Japanese politics. The construction industry provides votes for politicians because, as the largest industry in Japan, it employs some five million people, far surpassing the number of Japan's agricultural workers. During elections, votes provided by the construction industry are known to be highly reliable. Employees at construction companies vote in a block like families, and they make sure that everyone gets out to vote.

Public works projects are also crucial to the re-election campaigns of the heads of local governments. For this reason, such local politicians organize local support for the reelection campaign of a national government politician who will help bring public works projects to their community. That is why a politician who is appointed construction minister gets a boost in votes during elections, as shown in the following examples (percent increase refers to the total votes received in an election compared to the number received in an election prior to tenure as construction minister):

Year	Name and Electoral District	Percent increase
1969	Tsubokawa Shinzo (All-Prefecture District, Fukui Prefecture)	13.6
1972	Kimura Takeo (1st District, Yamagata Prefecture)	35.8
1976	Chuma Tatsui (2nd District, Kagoshima Prefecture)	53.2
1979	Tokai Motosaburo (3rd District, Hyogo Prefecture)	21.0
1980	Watanabe Eiichi (2nd District, Gifu Prefecture)	18.4

Ministry of Construction bureaucrats have repeatedly told the media that politicians do not build roads or bridges in their home districts just because they are construction *zoku* legislators or construction ministers. However, their formulaic defense is highly questionable, especially in light of what Kanemaru, the former leading construction *zoku* legislator, writes in his memoirs:

> I learned what to do as a construction minister by imitating my predecessor, Mr. Hori Shigeru. When Mr. Hori was construction minister, I was a ranking member of the Construction Committee in the House of Representatives. One day, I asked, "Mr. Hori, would you like to visit Mount Minobu[site of a Nichiren Sect Buddhist temple] in my hometown with me?" Mr. Hori belonged to the Honganji temple [a True Pure Land Sect temple], and so, as expected, he declined. However, I had really wanted to show him the suspension bridge at Mount Fuji on the

way to Mount Minobu. The toll bridge, built by a private railroad called Minobu Railways, was quite old, and I wanted it fixed. So I willfully persuaded Mr. Hori to go with me to Mount Minobu. As we were crossing the bridge, I asked Mr. Hori, "Dear Construction Minister, please replace this bridge for us." He briefly smirked at the ingenuity of my tactics. But immediately he assumed again his usual serious look, and said to an accompanying official, who was either a top-level official at the Road Bureau or the Minister's Secretariat, 'Well, this is certainly a dangerous bridge. Why don't we fix it?' 'Yes, sir,' said the official, and the construction of a new bridge began the following year. What a difference political power makes. I was quite impressed.

Kanemaru had imitated Hori's tactics, and it is no wonder that construction *zoku* legislators and construction ministers in turn imitated Kanemaru, their leader. The Ministry of Construction has earned the nickname of the "Muscle Man Agency" or the "Hammer Agency," through its reputation for primarily focusing its energies on winning large budgets for construction projects rather than engaging in policy debates. It is because of this focus that the ministry puts greater emphasis upon negotiations with the Budget Bureau than do other agencies. The ministry maintains ties with skillful politicians to gain substantial concessions from the Budget Bureau; thus it has been close to the group led by prime ministers Sato Eisaku, Tanaka Kakuei, and then Takeshita Hoboru, which controlled major LDP factions for years.

Unabashed Links to Diet Members. In order to understand the importance of this group, it is necessary to give a brief history of Ministry of Construction leadership battles. Prior to coming under the control of the Sato faction, led by Sato Eisaku, Ministry of Construction bureaucrats had been humiliated by Kono Ichiro, their former minister and Sato's rival in the race to succeed Prime Minister Ikeda Hayato.

Kono Ichiro became construction minister in 1962 during the second term of the Ikeda administration. For top positions in his ministry he recruited from among National Police Agency officials because, in his words, "there were no qualified personnel within the Ministry of Construction to choose from." Kono shocked construction bureaucrats by appointing Yamamoto Yukio, then deputy chief of the Osaka Prefecture Police, as director-general of the Minister's Secretariat. (Later, Yamamoto would become an LDP Diet member and then Home Affairs minister.) Hirai Manabu, a deputy director general at the Tokyo Metropolitan Police Board, was appointed chief of the Road Bureau. Machida Mitsuru, head of Police Administration at the National Police Agency, was appointed chief of the Planning Bureau. Furthermore, Kono offered an ultimatum to top construction officials: "I don't give a damn what you have done before I came here. Stay if you want to work with me. Leave if you do not want to cooperate or are not competent for the job." Two important construction officials (Kawakita Masaharu, who was known as an authority on roads, and Takano Tsutomu) resigned. Kono's reign at the Ministry of Construction lasted for a brief two and a half years. Meanwhile, Prime Minister Ikeda resigned due to illness, and Sato Eisaku, Ikeda's hand-picked successor, formed a new administration in November 1964. In July 1965, Construction Minister Kono died suddenly. His legacy and personnel appointments had made a deep impression on construction bureaucrats long after his death.

After enduring Kono's "abuse," construction bureaucrats quickly approached the Sato faction as soon as Sato became prime minister. Sato soon appointed one of his cronies as minister of construction (the home base of his former rival and the government post with the deepest sources of money and votes). The Sato administration sat at the helm for over seven years and appointed a succession of seven construction ministers with eight terms. With the exception of Nemoto Ryutaro, who was of the Sonoda faction, all these construction ministers were considered especially close to Sato even within the closely-knit Sato faction: Setoyama Mitsuo, Hashimoto Tomisaburo, Nishimura Eiichi, Hori Shigeru, Tsubokawa Shinzo, and Nishimura Eiichi (two terms). Meanwhile, three leaders of the Sato faction, namely Tanaka Kakuei, Nikaido Susumu, and Tamura Hajime, became increasingly influential in the Ministry of Construction through their LDP posts.

In 1972, Tanaka prevailed over Fukuda Takeo in the battle to succeed Sato as prime minister. While in charge, he also appointed his close associates to the post of construction minister just as his predecessor had. Tanaka appointed a total of four construction ministers, all from the Tanaka faction: Kimura Takeo, Kanemaru Shin, Kameoka Takao, and Ozawa Tatsuo. Not once did Tanaka allow another political faction to occupy the construction minister post which added to his reputation as the most skilled manipulator of bureaucrats at the Ministry of Construction. Over the course of several interviews, Tanaka explained his negotiation style:

> Government officials are human computers; politicians set directions for them. Politicians who cannot set directions are beneath officials. If you work with an official once, relations will last a lifetime. At first you fight with the official, who typically responds with 'Why should I listen to you?' You then tell the official, 'It's government by party rule. When you become a director-general, you will have use for me.' The official then will think about it, and come to his senses. The official will then come to you.
>
> The Ministry of Finance used to be dominant in policy making; they practically controlled policy through their budget-making power. Nowadays, however, the Ministry of Finance is having a hard time because there is not as much money to go around. The finance people will admit to you, 'We are not a policy-making agency.' At that point, a new policy is made if agencies and the LDP Political Council can strike a deal. The money for that policy is raised by a pay-as-you-go system. Whether we like it or not, the concept of pay-as-you-go will be the foundation of public policy from now on.

Tanaka has repeatedly stated that it was he who drafted, and then had the Diet pass, such important legislation related to the Ministry of Construction as the Public Housing Act, the Road Act with its three new taxes (the gasoline tax, highway toll tax, and automobile weight tax), the Total National Land Development Act, and the Law to Encourage the Construction of Expressways. In other words, Tanaka wanted to emphasize that construction bureaucrats were bound to him and should listen to him for their own sake because it was he who had persuaded the Ministry of Finance's Budget Bureau to set money aside for these new laws.

After Tanaka's political downfall, the leadership of the Tanaka faction was assumed by Takeshita Noboru. The reign of the political factions led by Sato, Tanaka, and Takeshita, over the Ministry of Construction continued for years under various administrations, with the exception of the Nakasone administration. When Nakasone Yasuhiro became prime minister in 1982, his administration was nicknamed the "Tanakasone (from Tanaka and Nakasone) administration" because its survival was so dependent on support from the Tanaka faction. The first-term Nakasone administration had to appoint a Tanaka faction candidate, Utsumi Hideo, as construction minister. However, as soon as Utsumi's grasp on power looked secure, Prime Minister Nakasone replaced him with legislators from his own faction; beginning with his second term in 1984, Nakasone appointed three from his faction in a row: Kibe Yoshiaki, Eto Takami and Amano Mitsuharu. The Nakasone faction also managed to have one of its own, Ochi Ihei, appointed construction minister during the administration of Takeshita Noboru, who succeeded Nakasone, but its influence over the Ministry of Construction was on the decline. The Takeshita faction, led successively by prime ministers Sato, Tanaka, and Takeshita, and the largest faction within the LDP, had regained its control of construction *zoku* legislators.

Both Kanemaru Shin and Takeshita Noboru headed the Takeshita faction, but they exercised their influence over construction bureaucrats in different ways. Takeshita was revered by finance bureaucrats who called him, "God, Buddha, and Mr. Takeshita"; he would soon show himself capable of strong-arming the Budget Bureau into accepting the Ministry of Construction's demands. Moreover, if Takeshita's many agency connections were fully used, they would provide construction bureaucrats with invaluable help. In short, Takeshita exercised influence throughout the bureaucratic system.

Kanemaru, on the other hand, was known to have had the firm support of powerful construction *zoku* legislators, as is illustrated in the following anecdote. The issue of *dango*, the bid-rigging practice by construction firms, who form cartels and keep newcomers from bidding for construction projects, came under public criticism in early 1982, shortly before Nakasone came to power. Kanemaru and Amano

Mitsuharu, who was a member of the Nakasone faction but regarded as a secret Kanemaru sympathizer, summoned Inoue Takashi, a Diet member and former administrative vice-minister for construction. Kanemaru, Amano, and Inoue decided to set up a subcommittee within the LDP's committee on construction to address the *dango* issue, and Inoue agreed to head the subcommittee. Kanemaru said to the other two, "I will take care of the remaining top appointments." A few days later, Kanemaru appointed Tamaki Kazuo as subcommittee chairman and Eto Takami as vice chairman. Since construction *zoku* legislators were trying to control the subcommittee, they were surprised by the appointments of two politicians not known for their connections to the construction industry, but few complained and they kept their faith in Kanemaru's reputation. Why did Kanemaru pick Tamaki and Eto? First of all, he considered Tamaki persuasive. Second, combining Tamaki with Yamanaka Sadanori, an expert on the FTC that was investigating the *dango* issue, proved to benefit the Ministry of Construction. Bureaucrats in Kasumigaseki still say that Kanemaru was astute in his personnel selection.

Besides Kanemaru and Takeshita, there were other influential politicians in various fields within the Ministry of Construction's jurisdiction. Amano Mitsuharu was considered influential in the field of road construction, Watanabe Eiichi in housing, and Tamura Hajime in sewage systems. However, a new generation of leadership was quickly emerging. One of the possible new leaders of construction *zoku* legislators was Ozawa Ichiro, former LDP secretary-general and now head of the new Japan Renewal Party, who came to the political forefront after serving as Prime Minister Takeshita's special envoy to the U.S. in March 1988. Prime Minister Takeshita and Kanemaru strongly supported Ozawa. As vice Cabinet secretary of the Cabinet Secretariat, Ozawa discussed with the Americans the issue of opening up the construction market in Japan. To reach an agreement on this issue, which was increasingly poisoning relations between the two countries, Ozawa held three sessions of talks that lasted a total of fourteen hours with Deputy U.S. Trade Representative Michael Smith. More importantly, Ozawa proved himself a skillful politician for reducing a far-reaching U.S. demand to open the Japanese construction market into "a range of businesses to be opened to American companies," which was a matter of degree.

But Ministry of Construction bureaucrats, however, do not really care who the leader of construction *zoku* legislators is, just as long as he holds an important position in the party in power and can get concessions from the Budget Bureau on behalf of the Ministry of Construction, and does not interfere with their personnel management as Kono Ichiro did. While politicians rise and fall, bureaucrats always survive as a group, even when they look like they are being abused by politicians. Ministry of Construction bureaucrats just have to find the right politician who will faithfully carry out Kanemaru's agreement to "invest 430 trillion yen in infrastructure." It was often said in the LDP that "he who controls the construction *zoku* legislators reigns." There is an element of truth to this statement, but the changes in construction *zoku* leaders suggests that it would be more accurate to say, "he who has real power controls the construction *zoku* legislators."

The Ministry of Transport: A State of Anarchy

When an official from the Ministry of Transport took up his new post as road transport chief at the District Transport Bureau he found that unlicensed "white buses" were being allowed to operate completely without restraint. (These are analogous to the illegal taxis that are known from the color of their noncommercial license plates as "white taxis.") Complaints were coming in from licensed local bus companies, and so this official asked the prefectural police department to crack down on the operators. However, the police official that he spoke to turned down his request. "The fact is," he said, "we ourselves use 'white buses' to transport police officers between their dormitories and police stations. Under these circumstances, we can't go after these buses just because they aren't operating by the letter of the law."

The transportation industry in general is one in which new services are constantly being introduced. Creativity and innovation abound: one thinks not only of these "white buses," but also of the parcel delivery services that sprang up so rapidly in the late 1970s. Unlike the industries that fall under the jurisdiction of MITI (industries such as steel, petroleum products, and automobiles), all of which are dominated by large companies, the transportation industry incudes businesses that can vary widely in shape and size. Anyone who owns a vehicle can start up a new business. More than one transport official has been heard to lament: "There are so many different kinds of business under our jurisdiction that we simply can't keep up with them all. Moreover, if we don't watch what we're doing when we move against some illegal business, we might have *yakuza* gangsters making threatening visits to our local offices, distributing leaflets, and influencing politicians to oppose our policies. It's a preposterous situation!" If the situation really is as these officials say, it is clear that the Ministry of Transport is unable to enforce existing laws.

A History of Scandal. In actuality, the Ministry of Transport has been given broad licensing powers, because the transportation industry has been recognized as "affecting public safety and people's lives." According to figures for 1991 from the Management and Coordination Agency, the Ministry of Transport was then the government's top licensing agency, having issued 1,966 licenses out of the total of 10,710 that were issued by all government agencies combined. There is no question that this gap between the ministry's administrative powers and actual state of affairs in the transportation industry has been an important factor in the birth of numerous scandals over the years.

The most obvious breach of public trust came in 1982, when former Prime Minister Tanaka Kakuei, still a powerful force in LDP politics, strong-armed the Ministry of Transport into giving priority to the Joetsu bullet train at the expense of competing railway projects. The Joetsu line traverses a region that includes Gunma and Niigata Prefectures, and Tanaka apparently decided to set up a station in his home district of Niigata to benefit himself and his constituency. Although public opinion strongly condemned Tanaka's ethics, the public prosecutors did not lift a finger against him. A high-ranking official from the Public Prosecutors Office's Special Investigation Division commented on such ties between transport administration and politicians: "The Public Prosecutors Office cannot interfere with such matters as where a new airport should be built, where a bullet train should run and what town should get a train station, even if the final decisions seem unfair and questionable. Those are political matters. There shouldn't be any problem as long as they were decided by standardized procedures."

However, a large number of post-World War II scandals have been directly linked to the Ministry of Transport. To give an idea of the vast nature of the scandals, consider the following summary:

Shipbuilding scandal of 1954. Leaders of the shipbuilding industry, including Yokota Aizaburo, president of the Yamashita Shipping Company, bribed Ministry of Transport officials and politicians to gain quotas for shipbuilding and pass laws favoring the industry. Justice Minister Inukai Takeshi used special authority to prevent the arrest of Sato Eisaku, then Secretary-General of the Liberal Party, one of the forerunners of the Liberal Democratic Party, and of Ikeda Hayato, then head of the Liberal Party's Political Council. An incumbent director-general of the Transport Minister's Secretariat was sentenced to two years in prison and three years probation. Three politicians were found guilty.

Land Transport scandal of 1954. Maruyama Takeji, director of the Teito Rapid Transit Authority, bribed politicians to favor his company during Diet deliberation over the construction of a Railroad Memorial Hall. Two politicians were found not guilty.

Bushu Railways scandal of 1961. Takijima Soichiro, founder of the Bushu Railways Company, bribed politicians to obtain the required railway licenses. Former Transport Minister Narahashi Wataru was found guilty.

Osaka Taxi scandal of 1967. Taxi industry leaders including Osaka Taxi Association chairman Tajima Taro bribed politicians to favor their industry during Diet deliberations over the gas and petroleum tax law that would have taxed liquefied petroleum gas (LPG), a fuel used for taxis. One politician was found guilty. Another politician died while on trial.

Lockheed scandal of 1976. To sell jet passenger aircraft of the Lockheed Corporation throughout Japan, president Hiyama Hiroshi of the Marubeni Corporation, among others, bribed Prime Minister Tanaka Kakuei to make procurement decisions in their favor. LDP Secretary-General Hashimoto Tomisaburo and Parliamentary Vice-Minister for Transport Sato Takayuki took bribes from President Wakasa Tokuji of All Nippon Airways. Sato was found guilty and his subsequent appeals were rejected.

There have been a number of other scandals with the ministry, including the gravel-shipping scandal of 1988, in which a Diet member from the Clean Government Party (Komeito), was convicted. Most recently, the Tokyo Sagawa Express scandal of 1992 implicated Kanemaru Shin, then the vice president of the governing LDP, who was accused of accepting 500 million yen in bribes from a shipping concern.

A House Divided. Why then is the Ministry of Transport incapable of reforming its policies to prevent so many scandals? Why are its officials so out of touch with the public? The primary problem lies with the Ministry of Transport's ineptness in appointing career officials. An influential transport bureaucrat who is regarded as a future candidate for administrative vice-minister remarked: "For the last few years, we have had our hands full with railroad and airport problems. We have no choice but to concentrate on such matters as a privatized Japan Railways, new bullet trains, Narita Airport, and the Kansai International Airport. Our agency's future depends on them. We cannot deny that we have been unable to assign capable officials to other tasks, but these areas are a priority for our ministry in general."

Indeed, in today's Ministry of Transport, there is a prevailing sense that officials in the Railway Bureau, Civil Aviation Bureau and Minister's Secretariat are more than a cut above the rest in their ministry. Officials considered brilliant among same-year entrants are chosen to work in these three divisions, and they are rarely sent to local transport bureaus or any other bureaus within the ministry. These transport officials consider themselves to be the backbone of the ministry. They have set themselves apart from their "lesser" peers, and tend to stay in their own "friendly circle."

This polarization within the ranks of the Ministry of Transport has done a great deal of internal damage. Those career bureaucrats left outside the "friendly circle" tend to become demoralized within the first ten years of their careers, as they are transferred from one post to another among the non-elite bureaus, local transport bureaus, local government offices and auxiliary organizations. This constant transfer of personnel impedes the ministry from functioning as a unified organization.

The ministry also lacks unity in terms of its jurisdiction. Founded in 1949 as a successor to the Ministry of Railways, it has acquired a mixed bag of responsibilities, including aviation and shipping administration (from the former Ministry of Communications), the administration of ports and harbors, automobile transport affairs and automobile safety (from the former Home Ministry), and even meteorological administration (from the Ministry of Education).

The Ministry of Transport is presently trying to bring itself together by assigning career officials to the bureaus originally under the jurisdiction of other agencies, but so far it has been largely unsuccessful in shaping up. In the Ports and Harbors Bureau, for example, of the twenty-two director posts under the director-general, only one is a career bureaucrat. The rest are technology officials independently recruited by the Ports and Harbors Bureau. The bureau's budget and policy making are off limits to other divisions of the Ministry of Transport, including the accounting section of the Minister's Secretariat. Other divisions of the Ministry of Transport, including the Maritime Technology and Safety Bureau, the Maritime Safety Agency, the Marine Accidents Inquiry Agency, and the Meteorological Agency, have also begun to act like independent sovereign kingdoms. Career bureaucrats outside the "friendly circle" have allied themselves with their division and will do anything it tells them to do. The Ministry of Transport is in a state of anarchy.

Further problems in the ministry have originated from inconsistencies in the appointment of transport officials. The Transport Policy

Bureau, which was founded by the Nakasone administration to transform the Ministry of Transport "from a licensing agency to a policy-making agency," is next to insignificant. According to a high-ranking transport official, the Transport Policy Bureau is superfluous and meaningless, "like a Minister's Secretariat number two." More importantly, the District Transport Bureau, a crucial division in terms of transport administration, is outside the "friendly circle" and left to operate on its own. "On the issue of licensing taxis, the Ministry of Transport does not give local bureaus any guidelines whatsoever. All local bureaus in turn leave the matter to the local industries. And if the industries want a license, the bureaus issue one," said a member of the rank and file who returned from a local district transport bureau to become a section chief at the Ministry of Transport. In other words, the Ministry of Transport not only fails to reevaluate a vast number of its licensing procedures and policies, but it also is indifferent to how licensing is administered at the local level.

Closely related to the Ministry of Transport's ignorance of and indifference to local matters is a blind reverence for laws. Its forerunner, the Ministry of Railways, had a habit of using a complicated "anthology of legal and written precedents" to settle matters related to the Japanese National Railways. Today's Ministry of Transport faithfully preserves this tradition through its powerful legal subdivision of the documentation section within the Minister's Secretariat. This small legal subsection, a group of approximately ten young officials, is nicknamed the "Crushers," because it constantly interferes with policy. Whenever a transport division or bureau proposes a new policy, the legal subsection responds with, "Who is going to take responsibility if the policy doesn't work? If you think it's going to work, prove it in detail," and subsequently starts the process of crushing the new idea. Otsuka Hideo, former chief of the Transport Policy Bureau has complained, "Once we wanted to start a new project, but the 'Crushers' informed us, 'It is unprecedented,' and killed the idea."

The legal subsection derives its power from the traditions set by the Ministry of Railways as well as from the status its members enjoy as being the brightest in their class. When he was the chief of the documentation section, former Director-General Nishimura Yasuo of the

Civil Aviation Bureau reportedly stated, "We have bright people in the documentation section. The District Transport Bureau is unworthy of them." The legal subsection officials and those who take temporary assignments at the Cabinet Legislation Bureau quickly move up the career ladder and constitute the bulk of the "friendly circle."

Continuous Setbacks. Criticism of the Ministry of Transport has been widely circulating in the bureaucracy. According to a high official at the Ministry of Construction, which is considered the Ministry of Transport's arch-rival: "If reorganization of Kasumigaseki does happen, the Ministry of Transport would be the first to be dismantled. We would be better off without such a hopelessly divided agency. The Ministry of Construction would be delighted to take over the Ministry of Transport's Ports and Harbors Bureau and merge it with our City Bureau." The transport officials themselves complain about how their own organization is run. Some even wonder if it can continue much longer in its present state.

These negative opinions have largely been supported by the Ministry of Transport's recent setbacks in Kasumigaseki's power struggles. What has loomed largest in critics' minds is the ministry's failure to contribute to the "Local Hub Cities Consolidation Act." Approved during a regular session of the Diet in 1992, this law proposed to alleviate the excessive concentration of government and industry functions in Tokyo by consolidating local hub cities and regions and reorganizing industrial facilities. From the summer of 1991, the Ministry of Home Affairs, the Ministry of Construction, MITI, and the National Land Agency had been jointly working on the bill that eventually became this law. Sensing the importance of the law, the Ministry of Transport, the Ministry of Posts and Telecommunications, and the Ministry of Agriculture, Forestry, and Fisheries moved to join the original four agencies to pass the bill. But while the latter two ministries succeeded in joining the group through the all-out efforts of their leaders and *zoku* legislators, the Ministry of Transport was left out.

Internal criticism over this defeat immediately erupted within the Ministry of Transport because the consolidation of hub cities would

have been closely related to areas already within the ministry's jurisdiction, namely trains, airports, ports and harbors. Some called for top
officials in the Minister's Secretariat and Transport Policy Bureau to
resign and take responsibility for the failure. Moreover, the ministry
had not submitted a single "budget-related bill" to the regular session
of the Diet in 1992. The approval of a ministry's budget is contingent
upon the disposition of such bills; therefore they are given priority by
the Cabinet Legislation Bureau, which scrutinizes all ministry-issued
bills. Bureaucrats work diligently on budget-related bills because they
must convince the ever-cautious Budget Bureau to approve new
spending. It was unprecedented for the Ministry of Transport not to
submit a single one. A former transport official commented: "The
failure to submit a budget-related bill means that the Ministry of
Transport will not make new policies for an entire year. Has the entire
agency become intellectually lazy?"

Another setback within the bureaucracy for the Ministry of
Transport is its continued retreat from the question of overseas development assistance (ODA), an item which other agencies have desper-
ately fought to win as part of their budget. Presently, ODA is handled
by the Ministry of Foreign Affairs, the Ministry of Finance, MITI, and
the Economic Planning Agency, but other agencies have been working diligently to join this group. The Ministry of Transport, too, had
been advocating that the present four-agency system be expanded into
an eight-agency system. However, during the late-1991 conference of
the Third Provisional Council for Administrative Reform, in hearings
on ODA and the agencies concerned with it, the council summoned,
in addition to the original four agencies, the Ministry of Posts and
Telecommunications, Ministry of Agriculture, Forestry, and Fisheries,
and the Ministry of Construction but not the Ministry of Transport.
This time again, diligent lobbying of the council members by the invited agencies had paid off, and the council had shut its door on the
Ministry of Transport.

In conclusion, how can the Ministry of Transport begin to turn
itself around? A serious reexamination of its internal management
and the placement of career officials would be the most obvious place
to begin.

The Public Prosecutors Office: Soft on Corruption?

In its investigation of the Tokyo Sagawa Express scandal of 1992, in which Kanemaru Shin, former vice president of the LDP, eventually admitted to accepting 500 million yen in bribes from the Tokyo Sagawa Express company, the Public Prosecutors Office was divided on how to proceed. Some incumbent officials criticized their own agency's summary conviction of Kanemaru Shin on charges of violating the Political Funds Regulation Act without a thorough investigation of the accused. Many in the media had reported that the Public Prosecutors Office convicted Kanemaru without questioning him because of the influence of top legal officials such as former Chief Public Prosecutor Okamura Yasutaka and former Administrative Vice Justice Minister Negoro Yasuchika, both of whom are alumni of the University of Kyoto (and members of the University of Kyoto faction). Sato Michio, chief prosecutor in Sapporo, wrote the following editorial on the case:

> Senior prosecutors have told their juniors, on many occasions and with numerous specific examples, that prosecutors have done their duty without surrendering to, and without fear from, the powers that be. I cannot emphasize enough how proud all public prosecutors are of themselves in their duties. Only that pride enables them to perform such a demanding and difficult job. The quest for truth means that one should do everything possible to get to the bottom of the matter and leave no stone unturned. It is a grave violation of professional ethics for a prosecutor, who is a representative of the public interest, to give up halfway in the search for the truth, and compromise with reality.

It would be wrong, however, to take Sato's criticism too much to heart and thus to assume that the Public Prosecutors Office suddenly compromised its own standards and became lenient on the Tokyo Sagawa Express scandal. Moreover, while a University of Kyoto faction may in fact exist within the Public Prosecutors Office, it would be too simplistic to link that faction to the manner in which the investigation was conducted. Why, then, did the Public Prosecutors Office respond to the scandal in such a halfhearted way? To find out, we need to examine a shift that occurred in the balance of power between the Public Prosecutors Office and the LDP after the Lockheed scandal of 1976.

The Lockheed Scandal: A Turning Point. The Lockheed scandal was triggered in February 1976, by a United States Senate subcommittee hearing on multinational corporations upon the testimony of the vice president of the Lockheed Corporation. According to his testimony, Lockheed gave officials and business executives in various countries, including Japan; bribes totaling 4.8 billion yen (approximately $14 million). Lockheed employed in Japan the shadowy political manipulator Kodama Yoshio, who, as a secret agent, procured purchases of Lockheed aircraft. Executives of the Marubeni Corporation and Osano Kenji, president of another corporation called Kokusai Kogyo, were also involved in the Lockheed scheme, and large sums of illicit money is believed to have circulated up to the government of Japan. The LDP headquarters was surprised to discover the names of Osano and Kodama in the media; close ties between Osano and former Prime Minister Tanaka Kakuei and between Kodama and Nakasone Yasuhiro, then LDP secretary-general, were allegedly a secret.

Around the time of this scandal, Watanabe Masaro, director of what was then called the Cabinet Research Office, was summoned by incumbent Prime Minister Miki Takeo to his private office in which the following conversation, according to Watanabe, took place:

Miki: Will the Lockheed scandal affect Japan? And if it does, what should we do?

Watanabe: We should leave it to the legal people.

Miki: Legal people?

Watanabe: I mean the National Police Agency and the Public Prosecutors Office.

Miki: Which one should we trust?

Watanabe: The Public Prosecutors Office would be better.

Miki: Would we be able to ask them how their investigation was conducted?

Watanabe: We certainly would not be able to ask the police because the National Public Safety Commission [the highest authority on police administration, whose members are elected by the public] is neutral when it comes to politics. In terms of the Public Prosecutors

Office, we might want to deal with them indirectly through the justice minister rather than talk directly with the chief public prosecutor. By the way, you may ask the police and the prosecutors for their opinions, but you must not tell them what you think, to avoid any improprieties.

There is no way of knowing how, if at all, this conversation affected the Public Prosecutors Office's investigation of the scandal. What is most notable however, is that Watanabe, who was a former National Police Agency bureaucrat, recommended that the Public Prosecutors Office, rather than his former agency, be put in charge of the investigation, or so he says.

Japanese law does not prohibit the police from investigating economic crime, nor does the law positively state that economic crime belongs in the domain of the Public Prosecutors Office. Article 2 of the Police Law states, "The police are responsible for protecting the lives and property of individuals; for the prevention, suppression, and investigation of crime; and the maintenance of public safety and order by such means as traffic control." Article 189, Section 2 of the Criminal Prosecution Act states, "Police officers are to investigate evidence and suspects if they think that a crime has been committed" putting the responsibility for the first stage of criminal investigation on the police. On the other hand, Article 6 of the Public Prosecutors Office Act merely states, "A public prosecutor is authorized to investigate any crime," a clause similar to Article 191 of the Criminal Prosecution Act.

The police headquarters in each prefecture has a Second Investigation Section, responsible for the investigation of economic crime. Throughout the nation, these sections employ proportionally many more investigators than other types of sections. On the other hand, the Special Investigative Division in Tokyo and Osaka each conduct investigations on their own, but they have only a combined total of fifty prosecutors in both offices.

Watanabe stated that the police did not have many officials with specialized knowledge of economics and law who would have the ability to investigate complex economic crimes, and that consequently, economic crime must be left to the Public Prosecutors Office. A former National Police Agency official had said: "The police cannot investigate economic crime scandals when the prosecutors monopolize the right to detain suspects. Even if the police proceeded with such an investigation, the Public Prosecutors Office would take it away or eliminate it."

However, a high-ranking official at the Public Prosecutors Office expressed a totally different view: "While the police protect the administration, the prosecutors protect the system. They are in different spheres. While the police can only act as the administration's 'security guard,' the Public Prosecutors Office people think that it is sometimes necessary to bring down the administration itself to do their duty." The official also said that two factors are necessary to bring down a system; one is that there be anti-establishment rebels. To be sure, the police can respond to that, but they are helpless in the face of another factor: a corrupting force within the administration itself. For example, corruption within the government of Ferdinand Marcos in the Philippines alienated the Filipino people and the police, which was the administration's "security guard," could not do anything to stem the tide of this corruption. In contrast, the Public Prosecutors Office goes after anyone, including incumbent public officials. That way, the government can regain the trust of the people and stabilize the regime, this official said.

Kawai Shintaro, the former chief prosecutor of the Osaka Superior Prosecutors Office who led the Special Investigation Division during its heyday in the late 1960s, agrees with the official quoted above. In his book, *The Prosecutors Office Reader*, he states: "The public prosecutors have never conducted the investigation and disposition of a case for the purpose of bringing down an administration. But an honest, fair investigation with facts and firm evidence and no political motive can sometimes cause an administration to collapse." He also writes that the public prosecutors conduct their own investigation to prosecute "cases that one cannot expect the police to investigate, such as internal corruption within the police, crimes involving complicated civil and commercial law, and crimes that the police should not investigate."

As seen above, the police and the public prosecutors have differing views on how to investigate scandals. Though it is doubtful whether the police could have probed the Lockheed case entirely on their own, the public prosecutors may not necessarily investigate a case even if they have "facts and evidence." For example, former Chief Prosecutor Ito Eiju, who took office in 1985, did not live up to the high expectations of his colleagues and the public. Considered one of the most brilliant prosecutors since early in his career, Ito was Kawai's protégé and had served in the Special Investigation Division for a record seven years. But he failed to prosecute a single "major scandal" during his tenure, and investigations of the following cases were canceled: the Heiwa Sogo Bank case in which the bank was accused of improper financing; the Mitsubishi Heavy Industries scandal; the alleged embezzlement of local taxes in the township of Karita in Fukuoka Prefecture; and the alleged attempt by the Kanagawa Prefecture Police to bug a Communist Party leader's house. Also, during the Recruit Incident, which was prosecuted under the tenure of Chief Prosecutor Maeda Hiroshi (Ito's successor), former Chief Cabinet Secretary Fujinami Takao and former Diet member Ikeda Katsuya of the Clean Government Party were indicted, but no politician was arrested. After the arrests of Tanaka Kakuei, Hashimoto Tomisaburo, and Sato Takayuki in the Lockheed scandal of 1976, the Public Prosecutors Office had not arrested a single politician until it arrested the LDP Diet member Abe Fumio, former director-general of the Hokkaido Development Agency, in the Kyowa incident of 1992.

This failure over a period of years to indict politicians was evidently due to changes in the attitudes of top public prosecutors, and not to a lack of facts and evidence. In the Lockheed scandal of 1976, then, what prompted the Public Prosecutors Office to arrest Tanaka, the former prime minister and the most powerful politician in the governing LDP? There are four possible reasons.

First, the prosecutors have always feared the justice minister's power of *shikiken*, that is, the minister's authority to stop arrests and thereby prevent the prosecution of politicians. They have bitter memories of incidents like the one in 1954 during the administration of

Yoshida Shigeru. The Public Prosecutors Office had issued warrants to arrest LDP Secretary-General Sato Eisaku and LDP Political Council Chairman Ikeda Hayato for their role in the shipbuilding industry scandal that year, but Justice Minister Inukai Takeshi, on behalf of Prime Minister Yoshida, used *shikiken* to prevent their arrest and suppress the case. In the Lockheed scandal, some LDP members wanted to block the arrest of Tanaka. Former Prime Minister Ohira Masayoshi reportedly said to an aide, "If I were the justice minister, I would use *shikiken* to stop that arrest." However, at the time of the arrest, Miki Takeo, Tanaka's arch-rival, was prime minister. Miki was not only anti-Tanaka but had proclaimed himself "Clean Miki." Had he authorized the use of *shikiken* to prevent Tanaka's arrest, he would have had to resign as prime minister and he would have lost his political viability. Miki and Justice Minister Inaba Osamu, who was a member of the Nakasone faction, must have told the public prosecutors that the justice minister would never use *shikiken* to protect Tanaka, and public prosecutors must have been able to launch their investigation only with this assurance.

Second, public opinion at that time was highly critical of the corruption in politics and business that was symbolized by politicians such as Tanaka. There was no question that the public would support the public prosecutors if they arrested him. Third, the facts and evidence of the case had been exposed overseas, particularly in the United States. Had the scandal only related to domestic factors, the facts and evidence would have remained solely in the hands of the public prosecutors, and crucial details would never have been made public. However, the documentation released by the U.S. Senate subcommittee on multinational corporations was extremely clear-cut and indicative of wrongdoing. The public prosecutors would have been hard-pressed to conceal the case.

The final reason for pursuing the Lockheed case was political considerations within the Public Prosecutors Office itself. In the Nittsu case of 1968, the Special Investigation Division had wanted to arrest Okura Seiichi, a member of the Social Democratic Party of Japan (SDPJ) of the House of Councillors, and Ikeda Shonosuke, an LDP member of the House of Representatives. However, Chief Prosecutor

Imoto Daikichi had refused to issue arrest warrants, which led to infighting between Imoto and the division. Since then, partly due to the aftermath of the Nittsu case, the Special Investigation Division had been out of the spotlight for eight years until the Lockheed scandal. At the same time, prosecution had become a very unpopular profession among legal apprentices. In 1975, only thirty-eight apprentices had applied for a prosecutor position while fifty was considered the minimum annual number of recruits necessary. To save the Public Prosecutors Office from such a crisis, young officials and public prosecutors from the Special Investigation Division argued, the public prosecutors must go after economic crime with vigor and stand up to political influence. When the Lockheed scandal broke out, a public prosecutor said to me: "This is a highly important and highly visible case that greatly interests the Japanese people. If the public prosecutors do not make a great enough effort, many will be driven to resign." Top officials at the office were well aware of this sense of urgency and must have regarded the Lockheed scandal as a perfect opportunity to turn themselves around. If the public prosecutors had put constraints on their investigation, the office itself would have been damaged. The all-out investigation of the Lockheed scandal seems to have helped to avert a crisis, at least temporarily: the number of applicants for prosecution increased to seventy-four in 1976.

Overshadowed by Political Influence. Although the Public Prosecutors Office was in effect rescued by the Lockheed scandal, Tanaka proved to be a formidable adversary after his conviction as his influence in the LDP unexpectedly increased. Claiming innocence, Tanaka greatly expanded his political faction and expected to prevail in court. At the time of the Miki administration, the Tanaka faction was at its height, with ninety-one members. Under the Fukuda and Ohira administrations, membership was decreasing in the aftermath of the scandal. However, his faction was on the rise again under the Suzuki administration, and it reached an unprecedented membership total of 118 in both houses of the Diet when the Nakasone administration was formed in late 1982.

Since the Suzuki years, Tanaka had controlled the appointment of Cabinet officials and important LDP posts. While the media were publicizing the Public Prosecutors' "total victory," Tanaka was undercutting the authority of the latter by appointing justice ministers sympathetic to him. His hand-picked justice ministers often openly criticized the Public Prosecutors Office. Justice Minister Furui claimed: "The prime minister has no authority to direct and supervise a commercial airline. The public prosecutors may have started the Lockheed investigation without considering such legal reasoning." Justice Minister Hatano even went so far as to say that "the investigation of the Lockheed scandal was illegal and a violation of the nonpartisanship of justice." He also suggested that, as a general principle, *shikiken* be used where party politics is concerned. Tanaka may have been more interested in wreaking revenge on the public prosecutors than achieving a victory in court. Known as the "Shadow Shogun," Tanaka reportedly curtailed the activities of the public prosecutors through these justice ministers, and he tried to weaken the public prosecutors at every opportunity, from the activities of the LDP Political Council to budget making.

If the Public Prosecutors Office had been a part of the judicial branch like the Supreme Court, it would not have been subject to Tanaka's reprisal. However, the Public Prosecutors Office is technically a part of the executive branch, albeit a quasi-judicial one. This office's basic necessities such as budget, law, and high official appointments were under the Cabinet, and thus the office could be indirectly controlled by a politician like Tanaka from behind the scenes. Tanaka's political manipulation of the Public Prosecutor's Office coincides with the relative weakness of the office under Chief Prosecutors Ito and Maeda. In his memoirs, Ito stated:

> Under the Constitution, Diet members are not subject to arrest while the Diet is in session unless the house they belong to agrees to have them arrested. Incidentally, the Diet Steering Committee, which issues arrest warrants on Diet members, has an unusual atmosphere. Regardless of party affiliation, members of this committee pose extremely tough questions to the justice minister or the chief of the Criminal Affairs Bureau, basically

asking the official under questioning why a particular Diet member should be arrested with a seemingly minor piece of evidence. When the official explains what the evidence is, when and where it was obtained, and so on, that information then goes to the member under suspicion in less than five minutes. It is really foolish to have all of one's cards face up.

In any case, I have come to the conclusion that it does absolutely no good for the investigation to request arrest warrants against Diet members. I think that the best remedy is to gather all the evidence that the members cannot deny, then finish the investigation with their voluntary appearance for questioning. I dealt with all my cases involving Diet members in this way.

What Ito really had in mind emerges from between the lines of these excerpts. First, it is quite strange that he, a career special investigation prosecutor, states, "it does absolutely no good for the investigation to request arrest warrants against Diet members." The special investigation prosecutors have been trying hard to arrest Diet members when necessary because it has been important in the investigation of economic crimes to restrain suspects and question them, and thus Ito's assertion that an arrest warrant "does absolutely no good" is simply untrue. In addition, his description of "an unusual atmosphere" makes no sense. The behavior of Diet members who serve on the committee does not seem to have particularly deteriorated in recent years, and they have been asking questions in the same manner for a long time. Ito appears to be describing the Steering Committee, but he may be referring to justice ministers picked by Tanaka. If one substitutes "justice ministers" for "Steering Committee," the passage would probably accurately describe relations between the public prosecutors and the justice ministers. In any case, "investigation with their voluntary appearance" sounds like Ito's admission of defeat.

Ever since Ito, the most experienced of the recent special investigation prosecutors, issued this "concession" in his memoirs, his successors have followed his suggestions. For instance in the Recruit Incident, the investigations of the Diet members Fujinami and Ikeda were done under "voluntary appearance," as Ito did with his cases. Incidentally, in November 1988, when the House of Representatives was in turmoil over the Recruit Incident, I met with Chief Prosecutor

Maeda Hiroshi, who made an intriguing remark: "The public prose-cutors are part of the Cabinet, so they will not try to destabilize the administration . . . Young people these days don't care about questions like 'what public prosecutors ideally should be.' I guess moral ques-tions have become out of fashion." Listening to him, I felt that there would be no more arrests of politicians, and I wrote that in a maga-zine article. It had been a surprise to hear him say that the public pros-ecutors "will not try to destabilize the administration," but he really startled me when he said, "moral questions are obsolete." During the Lockheed scandal, the prosecutors had made it through by posing "moral questions"; they had been confident that "If we public prose-cutors prove ourselves, future generations will follow our example." Now, however, Maeda went on to talk about various tangible issues such as working conditions and fringe benefits that involved the well-being of public prosecutors. It was clear that these were issues that required the cooperation of the Cabinet and the Diet, and that conse-quently, public prosecutors do not really want to antagonize politi-cians by "getting to the bottom of the matter."

Since Tanaka Kakuei's loss of political viability in the latter half of the Nakasone administration, the Takeshita faction, under the tri-umvirate of Takeshita Noboru, Kanemaru Shin, and Ozawa Ichiro, led the LDP-dominated government. This faction has mimicked the "Tanaka method" and picked four justice ministers of its own in an unbroken succession: from Hasegawa Shin in the Kaifu Toshiki administration to Tawara Shigeru in the Miyazawa Kiichi administra-tion. It seems fairly obvious that, during all this time, the public pros-ecutors' hands were tied, just as in the Tanaka era. With the collapse of the LDP and its subsequent loss of influence, the public prosecu-tors have been emboldened and have begun to prosecute politicians more severely without fear of political consequences.

The National Police Agency: A Quasi-military Organization

"The National Police Agency sticks its nose into everything these days. I guess they are trying to secure *amakudari* positions, which have become very scarce. If this trend continues, Japan will become a police state. I think all agencies need to make room for retired police officials so that they won't have to continue acting in this desperate way," comments a high official in the bureaucracy. Indeed, compared to the *amakudari* prospects enjoyed by retired officials of economic agencies such as MITI and the Ministry of Finance, there are few options for National Police Agency retirees. For instance, consider the list of new positions for the retired classmates of recently retired police official, Suzuki Ryoichi, who entered the agency in 1956: advisor to a medium-size insurance company; advisor to a large consumer electronics company; director of the Teito High Speed Transport Authority; trustee of the Japan Compact Car Association; vice president of Japan Game Card, Inc.; director of a road facilities council; advisor to a major commercial airline; advisor to a major advertising agency; trustee of the Hanshin Expressways Public Corporation, and so forth.

National Police Agency bureaucrats become prefecture police chiefs as early as in their mid-forties. This is a position of broad authority and most are invited almost daily to parties by business people, local politicians, interest groups, and prefectural legislature members. Police officials placed on assignment to local prefectures are so popular and highly-esteemed that "one-third return to the agency nearly alcoholic," an agency official said.

However, police officials receive very low-key retirement options considering the level of their power early in their careers. An executive at a medium-sized life insurance company says: "As a practice, we have hired former local police chiefs as advisors. But we don't know what to do with them. Retired finance officials are a boon to our business, and we can give them actual work to do, to a certain extent. But former police officials are next to useless. So we give them an office, a secretary, and a car, and have them keep a low profile until the next former police official arrives." Private companies tend to accept former bureaucrats if they come from a particular agency that is closely involved with their business through licensing and administrative guidance. Unless former bureaucrats have certain extraordinary skills or talents, companies are reluctant to accept them for reasons other than institutional connections.

Police administration, with a few exceptions such as traffic policing, "deals with the lowest elements of society," according to a high-ranking police official, thus retirees have no major *amakudari* prospects other than at security companies and investigative agencies. Consequently, retired Police Agency officials have resorted to creating new businesses such as the "Public Policy Research Council," a private-company consulting firm that became an issue in the Recruit Incident of 1988. Others were instrumental in introducing a prepaid card system for the pachinko gambling machine industry, thus securing *amakudari* prospects in a company that makes the card. The National Police Agency even invited itself into a conference of agencies convened to discuss ideas for the "Law to Encourage the Use of Recycled Resources," a recycling law that was created by the Diet in 1991. Whether the agency did so as an attempt to secure any *amakudari* prospects that might develop is unclear, but it is certain that the agency in recent years has been sticking its nose into administrative areas that seem hardly relevant to its jurisdiction.

A few years ago, in a discussion with several high police officials, I was told: "Police administration is greatly affected by other agencies, however, the National Police Agency should not interfere with other agencies' business. We should be content with simply being good 'minesweepers.'" ("Mines" were used as a metaphor for crime and other problems in society.) However, National Police Agency bureaucrats these days are not satisfied with simply "minesweeping" and have begun to interfere with policies designed to keep so-called threatening forces from creating trouble in the first place.

A Citizen Police Force? About a decade ago, an intruder managed to enter the bedroom of Queen Elizabeth in Buckingham Palace in England. Although the Queen was not injured, this incident exposed the vulnerability of security measures for the British Royal Family. Nevertheless, Scotland Yard, the metropolitan police of London, did not take any severe disciplinary actions against anyone; the authorities just replaced a few officers who were on duty at the Palace on the night of the incident with other officers.

What would happen if a similar incident occurred at the Imperial Palace in Japan? Not only the officers on duty at the Imperial Palace, but also the chief of the Police's Imperial Palace Division would be forced to resign, and even the Home Affairs minister, who also serves as chairman of the National Public Safety Commission, might be held accountable.

The difference in the degree of reaction between Japan and England comes not from the degree of importance attached to the respective royal families, but from the fundamental differences in the police systems of the two countries. In England, for instance, police officers do not hold the special status in the eyes of the citizenry that their counterparts do in Japan. The main function of their uniform is that it enables citizens to easily recognize them. Until recently, officers in Scotland Yard did not even carry a gun. Their top police officials are not automatically disciplined or fired for problems created by subordinate police officers when they are widely publicized in the media. The chief of Scotland Yard has stated, "police officers are just like any other people, and some of them happen to be crooks." The police in England have an open attitude about internal scandals and problems. The annual "Police White Paper" devotes a whole chapter to corruption among police officers by situation, citing disciplinary measures for offenders, and giving such details as whether they are to be fired, forced to take a pay cut, and so on. Police officers in England also have a right to form a labor union.

A police officers' right to organize has long been accepted as a part of life in Western nations, including the U.S. and France. In 1989, when the Soviet Union was near its demise, its military even formed a union. Japan, however, is a rarity among industrialized nations in that it does not let its police officers organize. Japan's police force in Japan differs from those in other countries in other aspects as well. Observers from the West and Southeast Asian nations have often visited Japan to learn more about what they assume to be the contribution of the police to public safety and low crime rates. Visitors praise the high conviction rates, the *koban,* or police box, system and the high standards of education and training for police officers. Some Asian nations, such as Singapore, have even adopted the *koban* system.

Contrary to outsiders' positive observations, however, the reality of the police in Japan is not a pretty picture. Problems abound: scandals created by police officers, an increasing number of unsolved criminal cases, the loss of the political impartiality of the police because of the transfer of top National Police Agency officials to political positions, and more. "If the present trend continues, we will have trouble governing our own police. Top officials in prefecture police forces and chiefs of police stations are busy placating their subordinates and are not concentrating on important cases," lamented an official who would later be a director-general of the National Police Agency. The major underlying realities of the police in Japan that contradicts the positive assessments of foreign observers are that the organizational structure of the police puts too much emphasis on national security and that the police squads, in the eyes of the Japanese people, are continuing to resemble a quasi-military organization.

Upon the founding of Scotland Yard, a famous debate was held over whether, if London were occupied by a foreign power, the police ought to fight the occupation army along with the Royal armed forces or continue policing citizens even under occupation? Scotland Yard chose the latter alternative, emphasizing the concept of a "citizen police" that would work under a regime of any political persuasion, even Communist. This meant that the organization would fundamentally remain apolitical. Most police organizations in Western nations are "citizen police" as opposed to "political police." The police in Japan, on the other hand, are most definitely "political police," although they call themselves a "citizen police." Few Police Agency officials expect a revolution by the Communists or any other group in Japan. Nevertheless, the organizational structure of the police has changed little in years, and a great deal of money and manpower go to security policing. Consequently, the police have been unable to keep up with changes in society as a whole and with increasingly complicated and diversified criminal activity. The emphasis on security policing contributes to defining Japan's police as a quasi-military organization.

There are major problems with this type of organizational structure. In particular, a quasi-military organization has little tolerance for dissent. When speaking as individuals, incumbent and former National Police Agency bureaucrats express their concern about these developments in the National Police Agency and offer quite innovative ideas for reform. However, as incumbent officials move up the career ladder, their reformist ideas evaporate. When I asked a former high police official, who had once given me a really compelling idea for reform, "why don't you ask your juniors to act on your idea?" he grimaced, saying that "a rule of thumb in bureaucracy is that retired officials don't tell incumbent ones what to do."

The Security Bureau, in charge of national security and public safety policing, is considered the real powerbase of the National Police Agency, and it has generally disregarded dissent in the agency. Gotoda Masaharu, former director-general of the Security Bureau and director-general of the National Police Agency, said: "There is no conflict between the Security and Criminal Investigation Bureaus, but the Security Bureau would never let go of capable personnel." In the bureaucracy, the agency division that keeps gaining personnel considered the most capable in their class (not necessarily the ones with the highest rank) has the real authority. That is why the Security Bureau, which has not been granted special status under the National Police Law but has acquired highly competent officials, has become the "mainstream" of the National Police Agency. On the other hand, the bureaus essential to a police force, such as the Traffic Bureau, the Criminal Investigation Bureau, and the Community Safety Bureau, have been ignored. Although those bureaus are the ones that deal most frequently with ordinary citizens, they have little say in the National Police Agency. The system is a far cry from being a "citizen police" force.

Incidentally, armed forces can maintain their cohesion not only because they have strict discipline but also because they are physically apart from civilian society. They nurture a sense of solidarity while living together for the purpose of "fighting the enemy." However, it is far more difficult to have unity in a police organization. The reasons behind this is that, first of all, with the exception of the special task forces and so on, most police forces are not, by definition, fighting units. Moreover, they do not know who the "enemy" is. For "political police," the enemy may be "the anti-Establishment," but such a concept cannot be enforced in the police as a whole. The Japanese police have the Community Safety and Traffic bureaus, divisions that are hardly fit to find a common enemy. If the police persisted in trying to find an adversary, it would be the Japanese people, which would pose a difficult paradox.

Another reason for the lack of solidarity in the Japanese police force is the fact that the approximately 260,000 police officers live in close proximity with ordinary people in both their professional and private lives. Community Safety and Criminal Investigation officials are particularly in close contact with civilians. Officers in *koban*, too, cannot work without communicating and interacting with local citizens. Moreover, police officers live just like ordinary citizens except for those who live in police dormitories. The police, unlike the military, are inseparable from civilian society; that is why, for better or worse, they are strongly influenced by all levels of society. While perhaps sounding just like the Chief of Scotland Yard, I believe that the occasional wrongdoing involving police officers is inevitable. At the same time, the police would lose the citizens' trust if they did not maintain higher ethical standards than the rest of the population.

While the Japanese police are aware of the need for high ethical standards, they do not publicly discuss it. There have been frequent scandals in the Prefecture Police administrations of the Kansai region, which includes Osaka, Hyogo, Kyoto and Shiga Prefectures. In one case in that region, a newly appointed Prefecture Police chief was forced to resign, taking responsibility for an incident that had occurred during his predecessor's tenure. The National Police Agency repeatedly apologizes for wrongdoing and talks of strengthened discipline and better training for officers. Unfortunately such policies, if taken to an extreme, could lead to a disregard for human rights of officers on duty. In an effort to avoid responsibility for its own problems, the solution arrived at by the National Police Agency is to impose military-like discipline on the rank and file. Prefecture Police leaders and station chiefs are preoccupied not with their true tasks but with personnel administration. They are like noncommissioned officers who are caught between demanding officers and rebellious privates.

Some officials have expressed other concerns for the quasi-military structure of the police. A high-ranking police official said, "I am sometimes frightened to see that this police organization, so strong and disciplined, is controlled unilaterally." A former director-general of the National Police Agency also said, "If the police try to create a "sovereign kingdom" like the Kanto-gun Army (the semi-independent division of the former Imperial Japanese Army in Manchuria), we may not be able to stop them."

Factional Struggles. In spite of problems within its ranks, bureaucrats of the National Police Agency are still preoccupied with achieving success within the bureaucracy. They half-jokingly categorize themselves into four types: the legal studies faction, the political science faction, the sociology faction, and the politics faction. Former National Police Agency Director-General Mitsui Osamu was known as a leading member of the legal studies faction. One must inevitably reach the conclusion that the police, being the guardian of law, maintain a strict observation of the law. However, Mitsui reportedly concentrated on measures to combat the Communists and did a great deal of research on legal problems caused by security policing. The legal studies faction keeps its distance from the LDP and keeps itself within the closed National Police Agency community.

The politics faction takes an approach opposite to the legal studies faction, and was quite cozy with the LDP. Many incumbent police bureaucrats have been critical of this questionable relationship. The politics faction includes politicians such as Gotoda Masaharu, former National Police Agency Director-General Suzuki Sadatoshi, former Tokyo Metropolitan Police Board Chief Shimoinaba Kokichi, former Tokyo Metropolitan Police Board Chief and Justice Minister Hatano Akira, and more. Former National Police Agency Director-General Asanuma Seitaro was not a politician, but he was considered quite close to the LDP's Ohira faction (now the Miyazawa faction) and was ostracized by incumbent police bureaucrats who were afraid not only of criticism of their association with Asanuma as a "violation of political impartiality," but also of having the entire agency viewed as a puppet of an LDP faction.

However, members of the legal studies and politics factions move up the career ladder faster than those in other police agency groups. Many studious legal studies members are valued for their ability to answer questions at the Diet and to negotiate with the Ministry of Justice and Public Prosecutors Office. Several former high-ranking police officials have deemed them "very dependable." On the other hand, while the politics faction is ostracized in the bureaucracy, it had clout under the one-party rule of the LDP. To gain personal contacts and money, the National Police Agency found it convenient to use the politics faction, which had connections to powerful LDP groups.

As a result of the stronger influence of the legal studies and politics factions, the political science and sociology factions, although attracting many young bureaucrats, fade away in the upper ranks. I once spoke to a few members of the sociology faction who, trying to be objective, made a few important points, such as: "The police should not expand their jurisdiction without limit. It should be made clear by law." Another: "We should reexamine the Police Officers Service Act. The current law may jeopardize the human rights of ordinary citizens." And still another: "Police officers should be allowed to organize, and the unilateral control of the police organization should be done away with."

It has been a few years since I last heard such remarks, but it appears evident that no new reforms are being seriously considered. Some of those sociology faction members have become high-ranking officials in the National Police Agency. One can only guess whether they are still interested in their reform ideas.

The Immigration Bureau: The Issue of Illegal Foreign Workers

In 1990, more than 10 million Japanese went abroad for the first time. In the same year, 3.5 million foreigners visited Japan, representing an increase of 17.4 percent from the previous year. Registered foreigners who have remained in Japan for more than ninety days number 1.08 million. Japan has finally entered the age of internationalization, though it remains to be seen what changes this will bring to Japanese society and culture.

One impact of internationalization is the growing problem of illegal foreign workers in Japan. A few years ago, there were reportedly more than 250,000 foreigners working in Japan in violation of the immigration law, which is formally called the Law on Departure from and Entry into Japan and Recognition of a Refugee Status. According to the Immigration Bureau of the Ministry of Justice, as of May 1991 more than 160,000 foreigners had overstayed their visa, more than eighty percent of whom were believed to be illegal workers. There were also at least 100,000 foreigners who had entered Japan as tourists or students to work illegally as "disguised workers." (As of November, 1993, 297,000 foreigners, a number comparable to the population of a medium-sized city, were working illegally at factories, bars, construction projects, and other service industries.)

The branches of the Ministry of Justice's Immigration Bureau located throughout the country prosecuted less than ten percent of the 250,000 illegal foreigners in half a year. Approximately 12,000 were prosecuted between January and June of 1991, 74.8 percent of whom were men. While the number represents an increase from 8,000 in 1986, but the Immigration Bureau is not able to keep up with the continuous increase of illegal workers. Compounding these issues, according to Ministry of Foreign Affairs officials, there is growing criticism of Japan in Asian and South American nations as a "country that exploits foreign labor with low pay and no social contract and kicks them out when they become burdensome." Even though Japan has improved medical and insurance coverage for foreign workers a little, if the many issues surrounding illegal foreign workers remain as unresolved and disorganized as they are, that criticism is likely to become more vocal, and resentment will increase.

The Crackdown that Never Was. How is the government, particularly the Immigration Bureau, addressing the issue of illegal foreign workers? In the bureaucracy, there are many administrative areas related to foreign labor: immigration, labor, industrial policy, welfare, education, and public peace preservation. They encompass virtually all agencies in Kasumigaseki. There is a monthly meeting of officials at the rank of director-general from seventeen agencies that addresses the issue. The only agencies not taking part in these conferences are the Hokkaido Development Agency, the Defense Agency, the Environment Agency, the Okinawa Development Agency, and the National Land Agency.

The government is responding cautiously by taking a stand against accepting foreign blue-collar workers, "considering the experiences of other countries with foreign labor problems and the possible effects to our country, including those to our labor market." The following agencies are considered the most vocal opponents against accepting foreign blue-collar workers: the National Police Agency, which believes it would have adverse effects on public safety; the Ministry of Labor, which fears for the future of Japan's labor force; and MITI, which believes it would damage prospects for structural reform of industry. Based on the government's overall policy, the current immigration law does not admit foreigners into Japan to engage in blue-collar employment. Blue-collar labor, however, is at present the primary source of illegal immigration, and the Immigration Bureau is responsible for enforcing the immigration law.

The Immigration Bureau is responsible for "management of departure from and arrival in Japan, the stay of foreigners in the country, recognition of refugee status, registration of foreigners, temporary shelters for foreigners, and managing local bureau branches." In 1986, an amendment to the law, "making basic plans for management of departure from and arrival in Japan," was added to the bureau's list of the responsibilities. In 1990, the bureau had 1,513 employees, an increase of fifty-two from the previous year. Under leadership of the Justice Minister's Secretariat, the Immigration Bureau has six sections: General Affairs, Policy, Arrival and Stay, Inspection, Security, and Registration, as well as one deputy director-general and a Refugee Recognition Office.

Local Immigration Bureau branches are divided into eight main divisions located in major cities, including Tokyo and Osaka; four subdivisions in other cities, including Yokohama and Narita; ninety-eight stations under the subdivisions; and two temporary shelters for foreigners in Omura and Yokohama. Immigration Bureau officials are classified into four types: immigration inspectors (777 employees), border guards (585), legal affairs officials under the bureau's director general and legal officers (151).

At the local branches, border guards handle the investigation, prosecution, and deportation of illegal foreigners. Border guards are chosen from successful candidates for the Border Guard Service Exam, and they are paid better than ordinary administrative officials in government because, like police officers, they belong to the public safety profession. They have ranks similar to those of the police and can carry arms with their superiors' permission.

However, 585 border guards are simply no match for 297,000 illegal foreigners scattered all across the country. Some police officers say that "even when a police officer reports an illegal foreigner to a local branch of the Immigration Bureau, the border guards often look the other way." A woman who runs a refuge for foreign workers in Yokohama also stated: "Border guards appear overworked. They often skip lunch and work late into the night. Perhaps for that reason, they often don't even bother to go after foreign workers who they know are illegal until they are pushed by their superiors. Some officers complain that there are simply too many illegal workers for them to handle." From 1981 to 1990, the number of people leaving and entering Japan increased by 160 percent and investigations on immigration law violations by nearly 1,200 percent. Meanwhile, Immigration Bureau personnel increased by only 8 percent, or 108. Border guards increased by a mere seven people.

The government as a whole has no comprehensive grasp of the broadening foreign worker issue. Furthermore, other agencies have consistently refused to cooperate with the Immigration Bureau. A "Report on the State of Foreign Labor," issued by the Administrative Inspection Bureau of the Management and Coordination Agency, cites examples of this lack of coordination. The Labor Standards Bureau of the Ministry of Labor is in a position to know the issue more extensively than anyone, but it has not conducted any serious investigation because "we treat foreigners and Japanese the same in respect to the Labor Standards Act." The Ministry of Construction and MITI are no better in comprehensively addressing the issue under their jurisdictions. The only exceptions are the Ministry of Agriculture, Forestry, and Fisheries, which investigates foreign crew members of fishing boats, and the Ministry of Transport, which investigates foreign crew members of cruise line ships and foreign pilots of airlines.

THE IMMIGRATION BUREAU 141

Article 62, Section 2 of the immigration law requires national and local public officials to notify the Immigration Bureau whenever they find any foreigner who illegally enters, stays, and engages in unauthorized activities, but this clause is rarely enforced. In 1990, out of the nearly 4,700 immigration-law-related accusations, 41.7 percent were brought by the Public Prosecutors Office; 29.2 percent by Prefecture Police organizations; 15.8 percent by correctional facilities such as prisons; 7.3 percent by the Maritime Safety Agency; 1.4 percent by municipalities such as cities, towns, and villages; and 4.5 percent by all the other government agencies combined. It is worth noting that municipalities were hardly cooperating with the provision, and the police were not reporting many cases either. A National Police Agency official says, "the Police Officers Service Act does not say that officers can check on people just because they look foreign." However, the police should have been able to report more cases of illegal foreigners, because of the many *koban* (police boxes) situated all over Japan that establish close ties to neighborhoods and neighborhood activities.

Officials in other agencies accuse the police of "neglecting their duty" to report illegal foreigners, but they themselves are not necessarily cooperating. In 1989, the Labor Standards Bureau issued a notice to its employees "not to report any employers except for those who are in serious violation of the Labor Standards Act or those who hire many illegal foreigners." The Ministry of Construction knows of illegal foreign workers in construction projects, but all it has done is to issue a notice to the construction industry to "strictly observe the immigration law." In other words, construction officials are beholden to the construction industry, which has shown itself willing to do anything to rectify its serious labor shortage. In any case, as long as the Immigration Bureau is ill-equipped to manage the growing issue of illegal foreign workers and as long as other agencies remain indifferent, the investigation of immigration law violators is not likely to go anywhere.

Ignored by Other Agencies. Why is such a state of neglect occurring within a division of the Ministry of Justice, the "guardian of law?" The background history of the Immigration Bureau provides some clues.

Founded in 1950 as an auxiliary organ of the Ministry of Foreign Affairs, the Immigration Agency's functions were transferred, two years later, to the Ministry of Justice to address the issue of illegal Korean immigrants at the time. The agency has been there ever since under the new name of the Immigration Bureau.

The Ministry of Foreign Affairs and the Public Prosecutors Office still dominate important positions in the Immigration Bureau. As a condition for the transfer of one of its administrative functions to the Ministry of Justice, the Ministry of Foreign Affairs demanded that the bureau's important posts from director-general down be filled by their officials. This condition has been observed; with the exception of the first director-general, who was a former Home Ministry bureaucrat, all director-generals have come from the Ministry of Foreign Affairs. The immigration inspector post in the bureau's policy section has also been reserved for Ministry of Foreign Affairs bureaucrats. Public prosecutors hold only the posts of vice-minister of the Director-General's Secretariat and security section chief.

Officials from these two agencies are reportedly distant and do not discuss such important matters as the Immigration Bureau's policy, budget, and personnel. The foreign affairs faction in the bureau tends to advocate the original agency's positions. For instance, in 1991, the Ministry of Justice, the Ministry of Foreign Affairs, the Ministry of Labor, and MITI disagreed on the founding of the International Training and Cooperation Organization. One faction was led by an official with strong ties to the Ministry of Foreign Affairs. A source has it that only three officials from the Immigration Bureau, namely the director-general, the general section chief and the policy section's immigration inspector, all of whom were from the Ministry of Foreign Affairs, took part in the debate on the creation of this foundation.

On the other hand, the public prosecutors faction does not seem to be involved in the actual management of the Immigration Bureau and does not interact with the other factions. When issues related to public peace preservation arise, such as that of Vietnamese boat refugees, the members of this faction, who include the vice-minister of the Justice Minister's Secretariat, the vice-minister of the Director-General's Secretariat and the security section chief, quietly discuss what to do among themselves. But they do nothing more outside their own faction.

With the Immigration Bureau divided into factions, it is no wonder that its does not do its job. A high-ranking National Police Agency official attributes the inadequacies of the bureau to "the public prosecutors' unwillingness to respect and work with politicians," but that does not appear to be the case. Even the Ministry of Justice leadership has been active in improving benefits for public prosecutors and an overhaul of the justice system. Bureaucrats of the Ministry of Justice and the Public Prosecutors Office have simply tended to ignore the Immigration Bureau.

While the two factions are preoccupied with their own agency's business, career Immigration Bureau officials who passed the Level I Examination for the National Civil Service, have assumed control. The highest-ranking immigration career official is the head of the Tokyo main division in the Otemachi district. Immigration Bureau career officials hold the posts of section chiefs of Policy, Arrival and Stay, Inspection, and Registration. By controlling the Tokyo main division, career officials thereby control immigration inspectors and security officers. By regulation, the Justice Minister's Secretariat has the right to decide personnel appointments of top Immigration Bureau officials, but the secretariat largely rubber stamps personnel nominations made by career immigration officials.

Meanwhile, the Immigration Bureau in Kasumigaseki and at its Tokyo main division in Otemachi are quietly, but increasingly, at odds with each other. In early 1990, a former head and general inspector at the bureau's Yokota branch station was arrested by the Tokyo Metropolitan Police Board for allegedly taking bribes from a Korean broker and attempting to allow 1,300 illegal foreigners to lengthen their stays in Japan. The Otemachi office had known about this case long before it became public, but it did not inform the Kasumigaseki office until the very end. Moreover, the presence of many so-called "disguised workers" who are purportedly at Japanese language schools has become an issue. However, bureau officials in the Kasumigaseki office have not cracked down on the issue, most likely because there are dozens of *amakudari* officials at those schools.

Dismayed by the present state of their agency, some immigration officials call it a "mosaic agency" or a "divided agency." Other agencies, aware of the Immigration Bureau's deep disorganization and frustrations, have consistently ignored it. The National Police Agency even says, "If the Ministry of Justice cannot handle immigration policy, then we will be happy to take over." Despite recent signs of improvement, the Immigration Bureau and related agencies are in chaos over the issue. The situation has got to stop: it is unacceptable for Japan to consistently ignore the issue of illegal foreign workers while failing to provide them with legal protection.

6

INDIFFERENCE OR REFORM?

Day and night
officials go after power
with or without good reason

—*the late Amaya Naohiro,
former vice-minister for International Affairs*

Conforming to the System

When it comes to their individual agency's self-interests, Japan's bureaucrats are chronically locked in power struggles. Even bureaucrats who are thought to reach balanced decisions become entrenched in power disputes, begin making the rounds of LDP political cronies, and focus their energies on peddling influence among industries. What an individual bureaucrat thinks makes no difference: if a bureaucrat at any level of authority acts in a manner contrary to their agency's policy, he should expect to be summarily dismissed. To make it in Kasumigaseki, a bureaucrat must draft new bills, win as large a budget as possible for his agency, and conspicuously rack up victories against other agencies in the struggle for power. Career advancement is an extremely competitive game. Consequently, a bureaucrat gains nothing from behaving with a conscience; such a bureaucrat is likely to lose promotion opportunities to same-year entrants, and younger officials will hold him in disdain.

Moving up in the bureaucracy is in many respects tougher than moving up in a large corporation. In the private sector, it is acceptable for workers to criticize how the business is run; as long as the employee performs reasonably well at work, he or she does not have to fear being dismissed. In the bureaucracy, however, arguments against an agency's methods are automatically rejected. An official who keeps opposing or criticizing agency policy will be either transferred to a low-profile post or banished to an interest group. On the other hand, a bureaucrat who is loyal to the agency will be well taken care of even if he or she does not attain a high-ranking position:

> "I am critical of how bureaucracy is run, but I had second thoughts when I attended the funeral of a high official at my agency. The agency took care of everything, from the funeral arrangements to ensuring the well-being of the surviving family members. I thought to myself, 'I don't have to worry about suddenly dying and leaving my family with nothing, as long as I stay with the agency.' I consider myself a stoic, but at that time I could not help feeling elated in my new-found sense of security."
>
> —*division chief at an economic agency*

In the bureaucracy, a sense of camaraderie and collective trust is cultivated among employees at every possible opportunity. All of the agencies sponsor get-togethers for same-year entrants. When those bureaucrats reach a certain age, and even after retirement, frequent banquets and reunions are annually arranged for the rest of their lives.

Unchanged for a Century
The tightly knit relationships formed within an agency have foundations in the Cabinet government system founded in 1885; the strength of these ties are essentially as strong as ever. The main reasons for

establishing the Cabinet system was to give the ministries increased independence in administration as well as to reduce the number of bureaucrats in order to improve efficiency. The document that codified the Cabinet system declares: "We hereby abolish the old system and institute the following ministries: Prime Minister, Imperial Household, Foreign Affairs, Home, Finance, Army, Navy, Justice, Education, Agriculture and Commerce, and Communications. Ministers of the aforementioned constitute the Cabinet." The Cabinet has basically remained the same, with the exception of eliminating the Ministry of the Army and Ministry of the Navy. Another major difference is that today's Ministry of Home Affairs, National Police Agency, Ministry of Health and Welfare, Ministry of Labor, and Ministry of Construction cover the former jurisdiction of the Home Ministry, which was abolished in 1947. Other changes include renaming the Ministry of Communications to the Ministry of Posts and Telecommunications and dividing the former Ministry of Agriculture and Commerce into MITI and the Ministry of Agriculture, Forestry and Fisheries.

Until the promulgation of the new Constitution of Japan in 1946, ministers did not hold collective accountability as a Cabinet; rather, they were individually accountable to the emperor. The prime minister was nothing more than a "first among equals," not the chief executive of the Cabinet. If a minister did not support the prime minister, the whole Cabinet could be forced to quit over a lack of consensus. For example, in 1901 when Ito Hirobumi, the first prime minister of Japan, who was then serving in his fourth term, attempted to fire Finance Minister Watanabe Kunitake he met the opposition of the finance officials, a move which led to the collapse of the Cabinet. There have been a number of other cases where the Cabinet collapsed, such as when the Ministry of the Army refused to follow Cabinet policy, most notably in the 1930s.

Without strong Cabinet leadership, each ministry came to view itself as a "sovereign kingdom." Moreover, the structure of Japan's prewar system of government legally supported and condoned their independence. The only check to the ministries was not the national legislature but the Privy Council, the emperor's highest advisory board. The Privy Council, made up of former bureaucrats, had virtually absolute power over the legislature. With the exception of laws concerning the imperial household, the Constitution of the Empire of Japan, general laws, treaties, and imperial decrees, the council had the de facto final say on all matters of public administration. In addition, the Privy Council periodically "coordinated" the ministries' functions "for the benefit of the bureaucracy as a whole."

The Privy Council was abolished after World War II, and the new Constitution of Japan unified the Cabinet body and strengthened the power of the prime minister. According to the Constitution, Chapter 5, Article 66, "The Cabinet, in the exercise of executive power, shall be collectively responsible to the Diet." Chapter 5, Article 68 states "The prime minister may remove the ministers of State as he chooses."

Despite the greatly increased power of the prime minister, the independence and sovereignty of the ministries has remained intact. The prime minister leads public administration solely upon policies decided through Cabinet meetings; it is considered beyond the prime minister's authority to make policies not approved by the Cabinet. According to Kataoka Hiromitsu, in his book *The Functions of the Cabinet and its Supporting Mechanism*:

> Each ministry is a self-contained hierarchy headed by a minister. The prime minister cannot bypass a minister to issue orders to lower-level officials in any ministry. If a minister steadfastly opposes the prime minister's policy, the prime minister must then either ask the minister to resign or withdraw the policy.

Under the current Constitution, each ministry has in essence remained a "sovereign kingdom." If anything, the ministries have become even more autonomous now that the Privy Council, their sole former oversight committee, has been abolished. Most of all, in the more than one hundred years since the founding of the Cabinet system, the ministries have amassed enormous power and influence, both tangible and intangible, including strong connections to the business community and lucrative *amakudari* prospects. Perhaps bureaucrats boast of their status and camaraderie because they have acquired a level of influence, prestige and power inaccessible to the ordinary citizen.

Perpetuating the Wartime System

Some argue that Japan's current economic system and Kasumiga-seki's administrative style are anachronisms inherited from the "wartime economic system" of World War II. According to Okazaki Tetsuji, assistant professor at the University of Tokyo:

> Much of what is known as the "Japanese-style economic system" was established during the roughly thirty-year period between the 1920s and the 1940s and especially through the wartime economy. World War II legitimized the government's bold reforms that could not have been implemented in peacetime . . . The Japanese government adopted a bureaucratic system similar to that of Nazi Germany and the former Soviet Union . . . The new system, called the "New Economic Order," was perfected between 1940 and 1942.

Sakaiya Taichi, a former MITI bureaucrat and at present a writer, and Noguchi Yukio, a former finance official and now a professor at Hitotsubashi University, have dubbed Japan's new economic system the "1941 system." In 1940–42, the bureaucracy made legal arrangements to promote the war effort, creating organizations such as the "Regulation Association" to facilitate the control of businesses and industries, as well as the "Patriotic Industry Association" to organize workers according to company, not job classification. Quite a few laws made in this period are still in effect. For example, Article 1 of the 1942 Food Control Act states: "The purpose of this law is to secure food resources for the people of Japan and stabilize the national economy." Article 1 of the 1942 Bank of Japan Act is unmistakably a wartime statement: "The Bank of Japan's mission is to maximize the nation's total economic power." It is expected that the amendment of these laws will pass the Diet by the end of 1995. Administrative guidance of industry and manufacturers may be said to be a legacy of World War II.

One would then naturally ask, to what extent did the seven-year allied occupation of Japan under the authority of the Supreme Commander for the Allied Powers (U.S. Army General Douglas MacArthur) change the administrative structure of Kasumigaseki?

The occupation government, which was known from MacArthur's title as SCAP, dismantled ministries such as the Army, Navy, Home, and Justice and awarded local governments greater authority, but these measures were intended to alter authoritarian institutions, such as the military and police, that were directly responsible for wartime violence. SCAP officials had once considered radical restructuring of the economic agencies, including moving the Ministry of Finance's Budget Bureau to the Cabinet. The ministries, however, were able to influence SCAP to allow them to function virtually unchanged. As a result, Japan's government agencies in the bureaucracy succeeded in retaining the "1941 system" by switching their primary objective from waging war to economic recovery.

MITI, the agency responsible for industry, trade, and small businesses, took the central role in the postwar economic recovery. During the war, what is now MITI was known as the Ministry of Military Procurement; it assumed its present name and shape in 1949. Former Justice Minister Furui Yoshimi, expressed skepticism of MITI's "transformation":

> SCAP considered the Special Higher Police, the Home Ministry's police organization used to investigate and control such political groups as the Communists, "Public Enemy Number One." They dismantled both the Special Higher Police and the Home Ministry in October 1945. Contrary to popular belief, however, not all divisions of the Home Ministry had cooperated with the military during the war. For example, the Local Bureau, forerunner of today's Ministry of Home Affairs, resisted military rule at every opportunity. But look at MITI's forerunner, the Ministry of Commerce and Industry, which not only enthusiastically supported the military but also renamed itself the Ministry of Military Procurement! MITI officials haven't changed a bit since. They are still ruthless opportunists.

Another vocal critic of MITI was former Prime Minister Yoshida Shigeru, a prewar diplomat who long served as prime minister in the post-war period and built the foundations of the "nonmilitary economic policy" that has guided Japan for nearly fifty years. Known as a liberal, Yoshida was not satisfied with the "planning" function of the

Economic Stability Administration, the agency responsible for allocating precious material resources in the tumultuous postwar period. Ohtake Hideo, a professor of Japanese politics at the University of Kyoto, provides an analysis of the Economic Stability Administration and MITI in the December 1986 issue of *NIRA*:

> The Economic Stability Administration was dismantled by the Yoshida administration and then restructured into the Economic Deliberative Agency (later the Economic Planning Agency), an agency in charge of economic analysis and forecasting but possessing no policy-making power. Another target of the Yoshida administration was the Ministry of Commerce and Industry, which had sent many of its personnel to the Economic Stability Administration, particularly its Planning Division. However, the Ministry of Commerce and Industry, now restructured into the Ministry of International Trade and Industry (MITI), was able to escape the full effect of these reforms. MITI gradually became adept at wielding influence over industry despite the imposition of personnel cuts and legal limitations on its power. Ironically, Yoshida's drastic measures intended to weaken MITI, if anything, only strengthened it. MITI shifted its tactics with industry from those of a rigid, inefficient "regulator" to those of a clever and effective "controller." Furthermore, thanks to Yoshida, MITI transformed itself from a shortsighted domestic agency to a nationalist agency with an international perspective; MITI became a key player in developing Japan's heavy and chemical industries, and it is significant that the development of these industries began upon the demise of the Economic Stability Administration and the Ministry of Commerce and Industry, both of which had called for a rigidly controlled economy. Yoshida had made sure that the Japanese economy would never become controlled and planned in the way that it had been during wartime.

Indeed, "opportunistic" MITI officials changed their administrative style, but even so, MITI's basic policy from the start seems to have been "to protect and promote industry according to MITI's blueprints." While their tactics may have become more discreet, their fondness for planning has not diminished since the prewar era. Since the late nineteenth century MITI's predecessors had been essential strategic players in Japan's national goals for industrial and economic development. After World War II, MITI replaced the Ministry of the Army and Ministry of Navy as the most prominent government agency, a status held until the 1960s. While MITI concentrated upon promoting its industries, other ministries, such as Finance, Posts and Telecommunications, Transport, Agriculture, Forestry, and Fisheries, and Health and Welfare, also joined in the race to encourage the growth of their respective fields. The Ministry of Finance promoted the banking, insurance and securities industries; the Ministry of Transport, sea, air, and land transport and shipbuilding; the Ministry of Posts and Telecommunications, broadcasting and communications; the Ministry of Agriculture, Forestry, and Fisheries, agriculture and the food industry; and the Ministry of Health and Welfare, the pharmaceutical industry. All these agencies undertook their pet projects independently without any national-level coordination.

Japanese industry developed so rapidly that by 1956 the government-issued White Paper on the Economy declared that the Japanese economy was "no longer in the postwar period." As far as economic recovery and industrial development were concerned, Kasumigaseki's "1941 system" worked much better after than it had during World War II.

However, Kasumigaseki's industrial policy hit a major dead-end in the early 1970s. Huge problems demanded attention: the poisoning of the environment, the growing economic gap between rural and urban areas, the deteriorating quality of life for urban residents, and the outbreak of foreign trade disputes. These problems were of such magnitude that they could not be solved as long as agencies continued to act as "sovereign kingdoms" and pursued their partisan agendas. The "1941 system," an institution whose time had seemed to pass, was ready for reassessment.

Despite a growing consensus for reform, Kasumigaseki refused to change. The agencies have continued to engage in ludicrous power struggles, despite several mechanisms installed by the government to coordinate among them, listed here.

1. Coordination of planning: Economic Planning Agency, Science and Technology Agency, Environment Agency.

2. Coordination of budgeting: Budget Bureau of the Ministry of Finance.
3. Coordination of personnel and organization: National Personnel Authority, Management and Coordination Agency's Personnel Bureau, and Administrative Management Bureau.

In addition, the Security Affairs Office, the Councillor's Office on Internal Affairs, and the Councillor's Office on External Affairs, were added to the Cabinet Secretariat during the Nakasone administration.

There have been few situations where these reform measures succeeded in coordinating among the various agencies. The Budget Bureau seeks to merely cut the agencies' budgets, and the coordination of planning, personnel, and organization, practically speaking, is defunct. The Nakasone administration was an exception. Prime Minister Nakasone Yasuhiro and Chief Cabinet Secretary Gotoda Masaharu, both former Home Ministry officials, effectively made use of the Cabinet system and focused on such important problems as administrative and financial reform. However, subsequent administrations have not continued with their successful reforms. The agencies are more autonomous than ever.

As long as coordination among agencies remains an elusive goal, reevaluation of the "1941 system" will likewise stay out of reach. A last ditch attempt to reform the bureaucracy was the formation of the Provisional Commission for Administrative Reform.

Resisting Reform
In 1961, the bill to establish a Provisional Commission for Administrative Reform was approved by the Diet. In February 1962, the First Provisional Commission was created under the direction of Sato Kiichiro, who was then chairman of Mitsui Bank. Ikeda Hayato was prime minister, and Japan was in midst of rapid economic growth. At this time, Kasumigaseki's "1941 system" was at its peak, but simultaneously its hypocrisy and drawbacks were becoming apparent.

In its September 1964 final report, the First Provisional Commission made the following argument:

The prime minister's position is far stronger under the current system than it was under the Constitution of the Empire of Japan. The prime minister can coordinate and adjust the administrative power of the entire government, however the auxiliary organizations that are intended to aid the prime minister in this function are extremely weak. At present, these supplementary organizations of the Cabinet and the prime minister are dispersed among the Cabinet Secretariat, the Prime Minister's Office, and their subdivisions; their functions and objectives are not clearly defined. Because of the absence of effective supplementary organizations, the Cabinet cannot exercise leadership in budget making, which in effect, amounts to policy making.

The First Provisional Commission proposed the following solutions:

1. Establishment of a "Cabinet Office."
2. Establishment of an "Assistant to the Cabinet."
3. Budget making should be primarily undertaken by the Cabinet, not the bureaucracy.
4. Establishment of a "Management and Coordination Agency."

None of those proposals were subsequently implemented because of the fierce opposition of the agencies. While several new agencies were later established through the bureaucracy's initiative, including the Environment Agency in 1971, the Okinawa Development Agency in 1972, and the National Land Agency in 1974, the existing agencies remained untouched. The First Provisional Commission thus managed to achieve few structural changes in the government.

A decade after the First Provisional Commission for Administrative Reform, the entrenched power struggles among agencies soon led to increased government spending and a huge budget deficit. Around 1975, budget shortfalls created a vicious circle: the budget could not be met without issuing national deficit financing bonds, and, in turn, additional government bonds were issued to help support the deficit financing bonds. Alarmed by these events the business community, led by Doko Toshio, the honorary chairman of the Federation of Economic Organizations, demanded administrative and financial reform of the government. With Doko as chairman, the Second Provisional Commission for Administrative Reform was created in 1981. The following is a brief chronology of the commission's activities, adapted from a 1992 article in the *Yomiuri Shimbun*:

1981

> *March 16*. Establishment of the Second Provisional Commission for Administrative Reform, with Doko Toshio as chairman.
>
> *July 10*. First report, on spending cuts and administrative structural reform.

1982

> *February 10*. Second report, on licensing reform.
>
> *July 30*. Third report, on reform guidelines, reform of administrative structure, and coordination of public corporations.

1983

> *February 28*. Fourth report, on the structure of reform proceedings.
>
> *March 14*. Fifth and final report, on changing ministerial subdivisions; blue-collar workers, public corporations; reform in budget, accounting, fiscal investment and loan program (FILP) and general administrative office work.
>
> *June 10*. Establishment of Commission for Rebuilding Japan National Railways.
>
> *July 1*. Establishment of First Provisional Council for the Promotion of Administrative Reform, with Doko Toshio as chairman.

1984

> *December 18*. Report on national involvement in local government and regulation reform.

1985

> *April 1*. Establishment of Nippon Telegraph and Telephone Corporation (NTT; formerly Nippon Telegraph and Telephone Public Corporation) and Japan Tobacco Corporation (formerly Japan Tobacco and Salt Public Corporation).

July 22. Report on coordinating functions of the Cabinet.

July 26. Report by Commission for Rebuilding Japan National Railways.

1986

June 10. Report on medical insurance and municipal administration.

1987

April 1. Report on transition of Japan National Railways to a new corporate form (breaking it up into six passenger railway corporations, such as Japan Freight Railways Corporation, and so on).

April 20. Establishment of Second Provisional Council for the Promotion of Administrative Reform, with Otsuki Bunpei as chairman.

1988

June 15. Report on land policy, land prices.

December 1. Report on deregulation.

1989

December 20. Report on relations between national and local government.

1990

April 18. Final report.

October 31. Establishment of Third Provisional Council for Administrative Reform, with Suzuki Eiji as chairman.

1991

July 4. Report on administrative reform in response to calls for internationalization of Japan and more emphasis on improving living standards of the Japanese people.

September 13. Report on reform in securities and financial industries (combating illegal trading practices).

December 12. Report on "fair and open" administrative practices.

While the Second Provisional Commission proceeded, administrations came and went, with Suzuki Zenko, Nakasone Yasuhiro, Takeshita Noboru, Uno Sosuke, Kaifu Toshiki, and Miyazawa Kiichi serving as prime minister. In this flux, only the Nakasone administration was serious about reform. It privatized the Japan National Railways and the Nippon Telegraph and Telephone Public Corporation (NTT), established the Management and Coordination Agency by combining the Administrative Management Agency with parts of the Prime Minister's Office, transformed the Ministry of Transport from a "licensing agency" to a "policy-making agency," and reformed the Cabinet Secretariat.

Kasumigaseki agencies fiercely resisted the Nakasone Administration's reform efforts. At the time, a high-ranking economic agency official expressed the common bureaucratic sentiment that "both Nakasone and Gotoda are former Home Ministry officials and all they care about is maintaining law and order at home. This country will go down the tubes if we let them do as they please." Several officials openly expressed outrage at Chief Cabinet Secretary Gotoda who they felt "betrayed the bureaucracy although he used to be a bureaucrat."

Not surprisingly, the bureaucracy welcomed the end of the Nakasone administration with open arms. The Takeshita Administration gave bureaucrats exactly what they wanted: considerable deceleration of reform. The death of Doko in 1988 meant an end to unity on the reform issue within the business community. Various scandals diverted attention from reform, such as the Recruit Incident in 1988, in which the Recruit Co., an information-industry company, was found to have bribed political, bureaucratic, and business leaders, leading to the downfall of the Takeshita administration. The "bursting" of the economic "bubble" further distracted the government from administrative and financial reform. Numerous bureaucrats, LDP politicians, and business leaders even attempted to do away with the Provisional Council for the Promotion of Administrative Reform, proclaiming it obsolete.

On September 9, 1992, Prime Minister Miyazawa asked the Third Provisional Council on Administrative Reform to consider "reevaluation of the functions of the public and private sectors" and "the defects of a vertical administrative system" with the intent of "helping the Japanese people attain the higher living standards that they deserve." The council immediately prepared for a comeback. In line with Prime Minister Miyazawa's request, of all the new experts appointed to the council, only two were former bureaucrats: Kawashima Hiromori, a former deputy chief Cabinet secretary and head of the Security Bureau at the National Police Agency, and Okina Kyujiro,˙ a former administrative vice-minister for Health and Welfare. This was a great improvement from previous councils, which had a ratio as high as twenty-three bureaucrats out of fifty-eight members. The council made it clear that the bureaucracy would not dictate its decisions.

Surprisingly, the media response was rather lukewarm towards the new council's moves. A *Yomiuri Shimbun* editorial on September 14, 1992, stated: "There is little hope for progress as the council debates the 'feasibility' of reform when bureaucrats only care about preserving the power within the domain of their own agencies. The council should disregard any short-term feasibility. Rather, we hope that the council considers a plan for an ideal administrative structure and presents bold ideas on how agencies may be abolished or consolidated." An *Asahi Shimbun* editorial of September 27, 1992, echoed this opinion: "The council's deliberations have emphasized 'feasibility' too often. The terms heretofore have practically been dictated by the agencies. It will succeed in producing a persuasive final report only if its members present their case without reservation and refuse to cave in under the bureaucracy's scrutiny."

The skeptical tone of these editorials seems to imply that agency reorganization simply will not happen. Indeed, it is impractical to expect the government to rid itself of the "1941 system": the all-powerful SCAP failed to do so, and the Nakasone administration managed to change only a small part. The editorials found in Japan's leading newspapers reflect the resignation of the Japanese people over reform of the bureaucracy, and do not necessarily provide an objective perspective. To many in Japan it seems naive and unrealistic to expect the government to undergo fundamental change.

Oddly enough, though, more and more high-ranking bureaucrats have begun to speak out in favor of reforming the bureaucracy. And standing at the forefront and yelling the loudest is MITI.

MITI's New Spirit of Cooperation

It has been nearly twenty years since MITI first became the object of sneering or the butt of bureaucratic jokes such as "both the world and Kasumigaseki would be at peace if the former had no Soviet Union and the latter had no MITI" or "MITI is Kasumigaseki's opposition party." However, as if to coincide with the collapse of the Soviet Union, MITI, which long has been involved in power struggles with other agencies, reportedly has begun a major self-transformation.

Without a doubt MITI was a major force in the bureaucracy throughout the postwar economic recovery period and the rapid economic growth period of the 1950s and 1960s. As Japan's industry grew extremely competitive worldwide, MITI's influence, ironically, began to wane. The government had gradually broadened its focus from industrial and economic development to other domestic issues such as welfare, education, foreign policy, and improving living conditions.

To cope with the reduction in its role and to survive the changes of time, MITI took action. First, it proclaimed itself "Kasumigaseki's think tank." Then it increased its involvement in policy areas partially supervised by other agencies. Since MITI's "industrial policy" covers such a diverse range of policy issues, and since MITI is also responsible for trade, general commerce, and small business, MITI's jurisdiction borders the jurisdiction of almost all the other agencies. It is no wonder that interagency turf wars persist.

In 1984 MITI suffered a major setback: it lost the battle against the Ministry of Posts and Telecommunications concerning the Value-Added Network (VAN) and was forced to concede its role as main authority of the Electronic Telecommunications Act. MITI is still smarting from the loss. To make matters worse, MITI soon thereafter lost other battles with *zoku* legislators who were deeply committed to other agencies' interests. A sense of crisis emerged among MITI bureaucrats, who seemed to be saying, "How will we get out of this mess? How should we change our policies?" The ministry grew increasingly isolated.

Building Alliances.   Beginning in the spring of 1991, MITI officials claimed to have made a breakthrough in developing new policies.

Hirose Katsusada, then at the Minister's Secretariat (presently head of the International Trade Administration Bureau), who had entered MITI in 1966, stated: "We at MITI seek to overcome the limitations stemming from vertical administration and to become more responsive to the needs of the Japanese people by building 'partial alliances' with other agencies." In other words, MITI proposed an end to infighting with other agencies over institutional prestige, pledging instead to cooperate with them on individual issues. Indeed, MITI submitted the following four important bills to the regular session of the Diet in 1991, all of which were made in cooperation with other agencies and all of which ended up being approved:

1. "Special measures to speed up preparations for special commercial development." This bill, which included neighborhood improvement measures and was submitted along with an amendment to the Large-scale Retail Stores Law, was drafted in cooperation with the Ministry of Home Affairs and the Ministry of Construction.
2. "Law concerning the improvement of employment management aimed at securing a labor force for small and medium enterprises." Drafted in cooperation with the Ministry of Labor.
3. "Law to encourage use of recycled resources." Law intended to administer the recycling and proper disposal of industrial waste. Drafted with the cooperation of six agencies, among them the Ministry of Finance, the Ministry of Agriculture, Forestry, and Fisheries, The Ministry of Transport, and the Environment Agency.
4. "Law to administer the proper investment of merchandise." Law aimed at developing a merchandise funding market. Drafted in cooperation with the Ministry of Finance and the Ministry of Agriculture, Forestry, and Fisheries.

Success in passing so many important laws in a single year, particularly with the other agencies' cooperation, was unprecedented in the history of MITI. Naito Masahisa, head of the Basic Industries Bureau at the time of interview, describes the background for the change in attitude:

> High officials in various agencies came to feel that post-World War II Japan lacked a sufficient perception of itself as a modern nation. The Persian Gulf Crisis intensified that feeling.
>
> These days there is an atmosphere of 'politicians revered, bureaucrats despised.' As well, the private sector is expanding both at home and abroad. The bureaucracy is clearly losing ground. Meanwhile, interagency disputes are getting out of control, and are sliding the agencies into a quagmire of ineffectiveness and inaction. Although Japan has long been led by bureaucracy, if present trends continue, I am afraid that bureaucracy will be more harm than help to the nation.
>
> Since the outbreak of the Persian Gulf Crisis, officials in Kasumigaseki have become anxious; they worry that the bureaucracy is losing its ability to run the country. From this crisis, a growing sentiment emerged that since Kasumigaseki is basically a homogeneous body of officials, why not cooperate and work together on the national agenda.

Naito believes that besides the four legislative successes described above, there is further concrete evidence of MITI's new cooperative attitude towards other agencies. For instance, interagency disputes over biotechnology jurisdiction among the Ministry of Agriculture, Forestry, and Fisheries (in charge of food), the Ministry of Health and Welfare (in charge of pharmaceuticals), and MITI (in charge of alcohol), were a common hindrance to development in the field. Now, there is cooperation among MITI, the Ministry of Agriculture, Forestry and Fisheries, and the Science and Technology Agency. When the Ministry of Agriculture, Forestry, and Fisheries founded a biotechnology research institute, MITI advised the industries under its jurisdiction to participate. MITI officials are also quick to point out that MITI has cooperated with the Ministry of Education on the issue of lifetime education and for three years has held regular conferences with the Ministry of Labor. This cooperative attitude would have been unthinkable with the MITI of yesteryear.

Interagency cooperation does not automatically materialize when high officials presiding over the different agencies reach a consensus.

How then did MITI form "partial alliances" with the other agencies? Top MITI officials first began by conducting frequent diplomatic exchanges with their counterparts at other agencies. For example, when MITI addressed the issue of neighborhood improvement and recycling, high-ranking bureaucrats met with their counterparts at the other agencies to develop a rapport. MITI next adopted a new attitude of flexible response, as when deciding what Diet committee a bill would be sent to, who would handle an audit by the Cabinet Legislation Bureau, what language or terminology would be used in writing bills, which agency would have jurisdiction over an area of policy, and so on.

Some MITI officials resisted cooperation with other agencies. Watanabe Osamu, who at the time he was interviewed was administrative vice-minister of MITI, after having been in charge of the "Law concerning the improvement of employment management aimed at securing a labor force for small and medium enterprises" when he was head of the Planning Department at the Small and Medium Enterprise Agency, spoke as follows: "The current administrative system makes agency coauthoring of a bill extremely difficult; it is even hard to decide what committee in the Diet one should forward a bill to. Cooperation requires every agency's trust and diligent efforts." Sakamoto Yoshihiro, head of the Basic Industries Bureau, described how MITI exercised its newfound flexibility in response to issues within its jurisdiction: "MITI officials decided to let the agencies hold on to their share of power. I was in charge of the 'merchandise fund' law. We set up a steering committee to discuss any disagreements and made sure to consider all opinions." Wakasugi Ryuhei, environmental policy division chief at the Environment Protection and Industrial Location Bureau and in charge of recycling legislation relates: "It was futile to attempt unanimous agreement, so we decided to compromise and let each other have a fair say. Thereby we succeeded beyond our original expectations." Finally, MITI officials practiced what they preached. To explain, MITI issued a report called "MITI Policy Making in the 1990s: A Long-term Vision" in August 1990. This report listed seven basic goals, the seventh being "to work in conjunction with other parts of the administrative structure." And MITI did exactly that.

Initially, the reaction of other agencies to MITI's "radical transformation" was mixed:

> "MITI officials no longer had enough work to do, so they became more discreet at trespassing into other agencies territories."
>
> —*division chief, Ministry of Posts and Telecommunications*

> "I cannot take MITI's words at face value. Can they be serious?"
>
> —*Budget Bureau official, Ministry of Finance*

> "I welcome MITI's change of heart. I would like to see an end to silly jurisdictional disputes."
>
> —*deputy minister, Ministry of Agriculture, Forestry, and Fisheries*

Two years after MITI's "transformation," other agencies have indicated a willingness to form "partial alliances." During the regular session of the Diet in 1992, the Ministry of Construction, MITI, the Ministry of Home Affairs, the Ministry of Posts and Telecommunications, the Ministry of Agriculture, Forestry, and Fisheries, and the National Land Agency jointly sponsored the "Local Key Cities Development Bill" and succeeded in getting it passed by the Diet. Although there was a small jurisdictional dispute whereby the Ministry of Transport was kept from co-sponsoring the bill, interagency cooperation to tackle pressing issues will be on the rise in the years to come.

The Fair Trade Commission: Does the Watchdog Have a Bite?

A young LDP legislator coldly dismissed MITI's new policy of "partial alliances" as "a desperate attempt by the bureaucracy to protect their turf . . . and an attempt to recover power." Perhaps he has a point. But we cannot become preoccupied with this, or we will lose sight of other important trends affecting Kasumigaseki, including a marked change in attitude toward the Fair Trade Commission (FTC). If Kasumigaseki is still deeply immersed in the "1941 system," the FTC theoretically is the only agency on the consumer's side. For years, the FTC has been victimized and scapegoated by the bureaucracy. Yet nowadays, bureaucrats from various agencies have begun to side with the FTC. A deputy minister of an important economic agency claims that he wants to "transfer to the FTC and undertake consumer administration to my heart's content." He is not an exception. Other bureaucrats have conspicuously begun to criticize the bureaucracy's single-minded concern with the interests of industries and the "producers." Slowly but surely, the bureaucrats are beginning to alter their frame of reference.

Recognizing its Authority. On December 17, 1991, the FTC "strongly cautioned" seven major commercial banks to end the practice of charging corporations fees for insider information in exchange for corporate bonds. The FTC also held hearings in 1991 on the banking industry's method of determining the short-term prime rate. The FTC's strong stance shocked the industry, largely because the banking community, which is under the Ministry of Finance's jurisdiction, had long been regarded off limits to the FTC's antitrust investigations. A major bank president stated: "We don't worry when the Ministry of Finance summons us, but the FTC is another story. Now the FTC even critiques how much a bank can charge in fees! If they continue to intrude, we won't be able to stay in the banking business." A high executive in a major securities company states: "Mr. Matsuno Nobuhiko, head of the Securities Bureau at the Ministry of Finance, once worked for the FTC. When he was at the FTC, he investigated us so thoroughly that he destroyed our revenue sources. As the FTC's oversight becomes even stricter, our future looks uncertain."

In 1991 the FTC also investigated the securities industry, which like the banking industry, had also been considered off limits to investigation of antitrust law violations. On November 20, 1991, the FTC issued a legally binding reprimand to four major securities companies, charging that the companies were engaging in illegal actions to make up for losses. The FTC interpreted the activity as an "unfair trading practice" prohibited under the Antimonopoly Law Article 19. The FTC further exercised its investigative authority in examining such fundamental issues as the domination of the market by these four major companies and their methods of determining underwriting commissions.

A financial executive of a major trading company commented that the FTC investigations have shaken the banking and securities industries: "Businesses have good reason to fear the FTC. An agency that has jurisdiction over industries may punish a company, but the agency ensures that the company will fare well. But the FTC, a quasi-judicial organization, could not care less if a company in violation of antitrust law later goes out of business." Furthermore, if a company were to receive a stiff criminal penalty for violating the Antimonopoly Law, the company's chief executive would be ineligible for government awards and excluded from participation in various deliberative councils. Top executives of major companies are particularly afraid of this sort of ostracization.

Companies fear the FTC not only because it has legal power but because it is being backed by pressure from the outside. In the U.S.–Japan Structural Impediments Initiative talks (SII), held beginning in 1989, the U.S. government has demanded that Japan strengthen its antitrust policy and the FTC. In the January 1992 SII talks, which followed summit meetings between the two countries' leaders, the Americans presented an additional twenty demands that Japan "improve its economic structure." Five of the twenty demands concerned antitrust policy, indicating Washington's strong interest in this issue.

The Japanese government accepted most of the U.S. demands and partially strengthened the Antimonopoly Law and its applications. It quadrupled surcharges, set up a report from the committee to discuss criminal suits with prosecutors, and increased by nearly 40 percent the personnel in the FTC investigative section in charge of antitrust law violations from 129 in 1990 to 178 in 1993. On March 2, 1992, the FTC released a report from the "Committee to Study Criminal Punishment of Antimonopoly Law Violators," recommending that the maximum fine against companies in violation of the Antimonopoly Law be increased from five million yen to several hundred million yen. Because of opposition from the LDP, which sided with corporations, the FTC's final version of the amendment to the Antimonopoly

Law set the maximum fine at 100 million yen. Nevertheless, recently the FTC has been more emphatic in its pursuit of specific issues. On November 6, 1991, just before its so-called intrusions into the previously off-limits realm of banking and securities, the FTC prosecuted eight plastic-wrap manufacturers who had allegedly formed a secret cartel. This was the FTC's first prosecution in seventeen years, since the 1974 incident involving the petroleum industry's secret cartel. The business world had smugly assumed that everything would be all right as long as the surcharge fine was paid upon the FTC's reprimand. In retrospect, they should have been aware that already by June 1990 the FTC had declared its intent to vigorously prosecute offenders. The trend is likely to continue. In September 1990, *The Economist* described Japan's FTC as "the watchdog that never bites," but we see the dog has begun to bare its fangs after all.

Reinventing Itself. There is a widespread, stubbornly held view within the bureaucracy that there are limits to the FTC's power. The following explanations are those most commonly given: the current FTC organization is weak in quantity (it has a relatively small number of 478 officials) and therefore quality; lacking *zoku* legislators of its own, the FTC has no impact on the other agencies' vertical administration; and the FTC is practically under the control of the Ministry of Finance, which is likely not to loosen its leash anytime soon.

First, let us examine the deficiencies of the FTC system since its founding in 1947 with the strong backing of the Allied Occupation. Initially, the FTC was comprised of an assortment of officials gathered from such agencies as the Ministry of Finance, MITI (then called the Ministry of Commerce and Industry), and the Ministry of Foreign Affairs. Soon, however, the number of officials who identified themselves primarily with the FTC gradually increased, and the agency came into its own. It had found its voice by the time the Antimonopoly Law was strengthened in 1977.

For a long time FTC recruitment numbers paled in comparison to those of other agencies. At most, three career officials a year were hired—in some years, none at all. While some of these recruits had excellent scores on the Level I Examination for the National Civil

Service, the majority were considered mediocre by Kasumigaseki standards. Moreover, since FTC officials were hired in such small numbers, many could reach, without contest, a rank equivalent to director-general. They reportedly did not have to study or compete at the same level as other bureaucrats. Thus it is a common belief among bureaucrats that a huge "ability gap" exists between FTC officials and their counterparts at other agencies. For instance, during the investigation of a cartel in the plastic-wrap industry, a public prosecutor asked an FTC official: "What specific damage resulted from the cartel? Who was injured? Why is the FTC indicting the plastic-wrap industry now?" The FTC official failed to give an adequate answer, even in response to such basic, straightforward questions.

FTC mediocrity became apparent in its handling of the "action plan" agreed on by the U.S. and Japan during the January 1992 summit meeting. The plan contained a clause requiring Japan to investigate the paper, glass, automobile, and auto parts keiretsu for "unfair trade practices." In the Kasumigaseki mind-set, this would have been a perfect time for an agency to prove its prowess, an opportunity any agency would kill for. However, the FTC hesitated to take on the task. According to a reporter covering the Ministry of Foreign Affairs, "the FTC feared the possibility that its investigation would fail to turn up any dirt in the automobile industry, and Washington would be furious." Such anecdotes quickly traveled throughout the Kasumigaseki community. As a result, almost all agencies now feel that the FTC habitually avoids confronting difficult issues and only works on easy ones to justify its own existence.

Furthermore, how does a lack of vertical administration and zoku legislators affect FTC power? When the FTC announced a plan to raise the maximum fine for antitrust law violators to several hundred million yen, Construction Minister Yamazaki Taku was the first to voice opposition, his rationale being that the FTC should not be raising fines when it had just quadrupled surcharges. Of course, Yamazaki's opposition was completely unfounded since fees and fines serve different purposes. The real purpose behind Yamazaki's objections to the hike in fines was that dango, the practice in which several construction companies form a cartel to keep other companies out of bidding, is a common practice in the construction industry—a clear-cut violation of the Antimonopoly Law—and that he feared that many construction companies would be indicted. But why, then, does the FTC look the other way when it comes to construction *dango*? According to one FTC official: "If [the FTC] made construction *dango* an issue, bidding prices would skyrocket, and construction work would be at a standstill." However, there is a more logical explanation for FTC inaction in the face of blatant antitrust violations on the part of the construction industry.

The prevalent belief in Kasumigaseki is that the FTC fails to confront the *dango* because it fears reprisals from the influential LDP construction *zoku* legislators. The FTC came under attack from LDP construction *zoku* legislators when it uncovered construction *dango* in Shizuoka Prefecture in 1981. This was the first case in which the FTC had issued a reprimand to the *dango*, and the construction *zoku* legislators immediately struck back by threatening to amend the Antimonopoly Law. Thoroughly subdued by the construction *zoku* legislators, the FTC failed to do anything about *dango* until 1988, when two incidents of *dango* cartel manipulation were revealed in the construction of the New Kansai International Airport and in the reconstruction of the U.S. military base in Yokosuka. It is no coincidence that both incidents concerned U.S. interests: the FTC was able to pursue these cases because of strong *gaiatsu*, or foreign pressure, from Washington.

Without *zoku* legislators of its own, to what extent can the FTC investigate the construction industry? Or the pharmaceutical industry, which is licensed and administered by the Ministry of Health and Welfare? Or land and sea transport, which is under the jurisdiction of the Ministry of Transport? Or even the agricultural cooperative associations (*nokyo*), which are under the jurisdiction of the Ministry of Agriculture, Forestry and Fisheries, and exempted from the Antimonopoly Law?

Moreover, how can the FTC act independently, when it is said to be under the control of the Ministry of Finance? The Ministry of Finance has sent more than ten officials to work in the FTC, including the FTC Chairman Kogayu Masami, as well as four incumbent career finance officials who occupied the deputy minister and planning section chief positions. Although the FTC has hired approximately forty officials from other agencies, Ministry of Finance officials have the largest representation by far. In fact, the position of FTC chairman has been filled by former Ministry of Finance officials for more than ten years. The Ministry of Finance's control is said to pervade the FTC.

Another detail that must not be overlooked is that the FTC is an auxiliary organization to the Prime Minister's Office. But while other auxiliary organizations such as the Defense Agency and Economic Planning Agency have been allotted a minister of state, the FTC and the Imperial Household Agency have not. In other words, they have been denied Cabinet membership. The FTC's chairman, its highest officer, has no right to attend Cabinet meetings. Instead, the chairman merely conveys the FTC's messages to the Cabinet through the chief Cabinet secretary.

On the other hand, the FTC chairman has virtually been granted dictatorial power within the FTC. The FTC central committee, consisting of the chairman and four additional members, decides matters by majority vote. The chairman presides over two daily meetings, one in the morning, the other in the afternoon. The agenda never includes items that the chairman opposes. The committee discusses everything, including FTC administration, personnel appointments, and the question of which issues related to antitrust law should be pursued. In effect, the chairman dominates the FTC.

As further evidence of the Ministry of Finance's influence over the FTC, the Secretary Division of the Finance Minister's Secretariat is said to covertly handle, on behalf of the FTC chairman, appointments of high-ranking FTC officials, central committee member appointments, political influence peddling, and negotiations with the prime minister's inner circle. As an example of how personnel at the FTC are easily manipulated by the Ministry of Finance, an influential FTC official explains why there was no FTC representative at the central committee from November 1991 to July 1992:

> To reclaim an committee seat that the a foreign affairs official used to occupy, a high-ranking foreign affairs official visited the

FTC chairman requesting that the seat be restored to his ministry. The FTC chairman complied with the request and eventually removed an FTC candidate from consideration for the next
vacancy in the central committee. This candidate was then found
an *amakudari* position in a public corporation by the Finance
Minister's Secretariat. The FTC chairman summoned the FTC
candidate, told him about the *amakudari* destination, and he
reluctantly accepted the position.

The long-term Ministry of Finance control of the FTC has caused
a number of problems, namely that the banking and securities industries have been made off limits to the FTC. An economic agency official who had worked for the FTC offers the following anecdote:
"When I was at the FTC, I said at a meeting that a particular securities industry business practice might be in violation of the
Antimonopoly Law and that we should investigate it. A high-ranking
FTC official who came from the Ministry of Finance threw me a
furious look. An FTC career official who agreed with me was later
demoted."

Because the Ministry of Finance's control over the FTC has been so
implicitly understood in Kasumigaseki for so long, bureaucrats were
indifferent when the FTC in 1991 suddenly intruded into "off-limits
areas," throwing the business world into a state of panic. The following opinions circulated in the bureaucracy:

- The FTC investigated the industries after careful consultation with the Ministry of Finance's Banking and Securities
  bureaus.
- The Ministry of Finance used the FTC to keep the banking
  and securities industries in check.
- Many inside the FTC administration were frustrated over
  the procedures and performance of the agency. For
  instance, the FTC's Economic Department investigated
  violations in the securities industry. But shouldn't the job
  have been relegated to its Investigation Department?
  Perhaps the Ministry of Finance's strong power over the
  FTC wouldn't permit that.

Is There Hope for the FTC? This situation, in which the FTC is hampered by limits to its power, will probably not last forever. Domestic and U.S. foreign pressure for change are becoming more insistent. For instance, on October 17, 1991, the FTC advised Nomura Securities to forego its control of its subsidiary, Nomura Land and Buildings. Nomura Securities had asked five other shareholding companies, including the Obayashi-Gumi and Sanwa Bank, not to sell Nomura Land and Buildings stock without Nomura Securities' permission. The FTC determined that this agreement violated the Antimonopoly Law.

This case reportedly was triggered by an "inside leak" by a Nomura Securities official to an FTC official. While more than 90 percent of the FTC cases have been instigated by tips from consumers and business partners, a growing number of cases originate from insider information derived from company employees. Whether this change reflects a trend among Japan's *sarariman* to act independently of their company remains to be seen. In any event, when credible "insider" information is conveyed to the FTC, it has no choice but to pursue the case.

A further explanation is that Kasumigaseki bureaucrats are in the midst of redefining themselves. Several bureaucrats whom I have interviewed intimated that the "the FTC is the only agency that can break the unhealthy ties between Japan's public and private sectors. I wish the FTC the best of luck." Such an opinion is bound to become more widespread, both within the bureaucracy and in the private sector.

Another sign of hope is that officials hired directly by the FTC are finally coming into their own. Many in Kasumigaseki believe that FTC career officials hired during and after the early 1970s are of a higher caliber than their predecessors. A major corporate executive states: "In meeting with up-and-coming FTC officials in a newly-formed 'study group' I have discovered that although they are not yet versed in the nuts and bolts of economic administration, they are open-minded, intelligent and fast learners." Kojima Masaoki, an influential businessman, who is hoping for the emergence of a stronger antitrust policy and is keeping an eye on the future of the FTC and Kasumigaseki says: "The FTC must get the media and academia on its side. It has a lot to learn."

Realizing a Vision of Change

In an interview a few years ago, Sakamoto Yoshihiro, former director-general of the Machinery and Information Industries Bureau at MITI, boldly remarked: "Does the international community accept Japan's policy of pursuing relentless industrial development while abandoning military affairs? I do not think so. I believe that we Japanese have to change our fundamental frame of reference. MITI's role in nurturing industrial development is no longer required. From now on, we must first consider what Japan should be as a modern nation and then reassess the role MITI should play." Long skeptical of the structure of the bureaucracy, Sakamoto has been a vocal advocate of fundamental reform. Even so, his opinion that MITI no longer needs to nurture industrial development is a bit surprising coming from within the bureaucracy. Another MITI official stated: "One of MITI's goals in forming partial alliances was to supplement the administrative element in agencies that are inefficient and ineffective. MITI is preparing for the possibility of agency reorganization in the future."

Not just those at MITI, but also top officials at other government agencies have begun to speak of merging, abolishing or reorganizing the bureaucracy:

> "The postwar administrative structure in Japan has responded to arising needs by establishing new agencies such as the Environment Agency. Because the old administrative structure was also preserved, administrative jurisdictions have become a labyrinthine maze. Vast amounts of energy are necessary to coordinate among the agencies. Top officials at all agencies feel it is necessary to scrap Japan's present administrative structure and rebuild it from scratch."
>
> —*a director-general, Ministry of Finance*

> "There is no need for the Ministry of Health and Welfare and the Ministry of Labor to set up separate shops; their areas of administration overlap in so many areas. We currently are discussing amongst ourselves the possibility of creating a

unified organization that consolidates all issues encompassing labor and the work environment. The new organizational structure might resemble the Social Bureau of the dismantled Home Ministry."

—a director-general, Ministry of Health and Welfare

"We should aggressively proceed with agency reorganization. For instance, we could combine MITI and the Ministry of Agriculture, Forestry, and Fisheries into a Ministry of Agriculture and Commerce, as in the pre-1945 system. On the domestic front, government would certainly be much more efficient if we could combine the National Land Agency, the Ministry of Construction, and the Ministry of Home Affairs into one organization."

—former deputy minister, Ministry of Home Affairs

"I am extremely enthusiastic about the future reorganization of agencies."

—a director-general, Management and Coordination Agency

These remarks have as their background the gradual deepening of the malaise pervading Kasumigaseki. As Naito Masahisa of MITI pointed out, "if present trends continue, Kasumigaseki may not be able to continue running the country." At the same time, in Kasumigaseki the reorganization of agencies is no longer deemed an imaginary dream, but a coming reality. Bureaucrats envision two catalysts that would aid in agency reorganization: the establishment of a "Ministry of the Environment" and the transfer of certain national government functions away from Tokyo.

Relocate the Capital. A proposal to transfer national government functions out of Tokyo was first made official in November 1990 when both houses of the Diet ratified a resolution that stated: "To prevent corruption all over the nation, the Diet and certain government functions should be moved outside of Tokyo." In August 1991, a "Special Committee on Transferring the Diet and Governmental Functions from Tokyo" was set up in both houses of the Diet. In December 1991, the prime minister's informal advisory group, "Council On the Relocation of Capital Functions" was established, with Hiraiwa Gaishi, the chairman of the Federation of Economic Organizations (Keidanren), presiding.

By late February 1992, the "Conference on the Relocation of Capital Functions," an advisory group to the National Land Agency director-general, issued a "Mid-term Report on Building a New Capital Focusing on Political and Administrative Functions." Following are some of the major points in the report:

1. The political and administrative functions of the national government shall be separated from the private economic sector in Tokyo. We intend to transfer only the political and administrative divisions, that is, the legislative, executive and judicial branches, away from Tokyo.
2. We will first transfer the Diet, followed by the gradual transfer of the other government agencies.
3. The new capital will have a population of 600,000, approximately the same as that of Hamamatsu [a coastal city in Shizuoka Prefecture]. The new capital will have an area of approximately 9,000 hectares [35.16 square miles], or, in other words, is larger than the area inside the loop of the Yamanote Line, which is 6,500 hectares [25.4 square miles].
4. The new capital should be at least 60 kilometers [33 miles] away from Tokyo. It should be environmentally sound, relatively free of natural disasters, plentiful in water supply, and adaptable to high-speed mass transit systems. The land for development should be affordable.

The initiative to relocate capital functions first began in the late 1950s, when many scholars, politicians, economic organizations, and others presented various ideas and suggestions. These initiatives died out; however, this time the situation seems different. Many bureaucrats believe that the transfer can actually happen, and even sooner than expected. "We want to decide the site for the new capital by 1995, start building by the late 1990s, and finish construction sometime between 2010 and 2020," said Murata Keijiro, chairman of the Special Committee in the House of Representatives. Murata's vision may not be too farfetched, as future Diet resolutions may reveal.

While Kasumigaseki bureaucrats were expected to fiercely oppose an attempt to transfer out capital functions, according to a National Land Agency survey conducted in February 1992 , shortly after the issuance of the "Mid-term Report," many bureaucrats surprisingly supported the transfer initiative: 83.7 percent of government agency division chiefs surveyed approved the transfer, as did 81 percent of the major company division chiefs, 80 percent of the people in the arts, 72.7 percent of the small and medium-sized business owners, and 50 percent of the housewives. Overall, 73.7 percent of those who participated in the survey supported the transfer. Bureaucrats were the most supportive of the idea, with 69 percent of the bureaucrats stating that they would move to the new capital with their families. Support for the idea may be due to the bureaucrats' hunger for change: "In Kasumigaseki, we need some major inspiration. Transferring out capital functions would force a reevaluation of administrative practices in government agencies. It would be a tremendous opportunity for a change." Division chiefs at MITI, the Ministry of Agriculture, Forestry and Fisheries, and the Ministry of Transport echoed this opinion.

If the Diet decides to build a new capital, legislators must immediately begin discussion on which agencies would be transferred, and with how many personnel. A Diet decision to officially transfer capital functions would lead to a fundamental reevaluation and reform of the structure and functions of what is Kasumigaseki today. That is why bureaucrats are beginning to think seriously that "agency reorganization is on the horizon."

A Ministry of the Environment? Another new idea that has been a greater cause for concern among bureaucrats than the possible moving of the capital is that of creating a Ministry of the Environment. Influential LDP politicians such as former Prime Minister Takeshita Noboru and former Finance Minister Hashimoto Ryutaro have advocated restructuring the Environment Agency into a Ministry of the Environment. In postwar Kasumigaseki, although several new agencies and the auxiliary organizations of the Prime Minister's Office were established, including the National Land Agency and the Environment Agency, not a single new ministry has been created. If the Environment Agency were to become a Ministry of the Environment, the Agency would absorb the environment-related divisions of MITI, the Ministry of Health and Welfare, the Ministry of Agriculture, Forestry, and Fisheries, and the Ministry of Construction. A number of bureaucrats believe that if that were to be accomplished and the new ministry were to take shape, then agency reorganization would already be well under way.

The idea of creating a Ministry of the Environment surfaced suddenly in November 1991 when the bureaucracy was busily preparing for the Earth Summit that was to be held in Brazil in June 1992. During the "Japan and the World" conference of the Third Provisional Council for Administrative Reform, the participants had argued for the strengthening of the Environment Agency. Nakamura Shozaburo of the Environment Agency responded to this by announcing: "Environmental protection is an urgent cause, and we need a system that can handle it. We should elevate the Environment Agency to a Ministry of the Environment." The media immediately took up Nakamura's call, and environmental interest groups raised their expectations.

Yet, the council final report of December 12, 1991, merely stated: "We must improve the planning and creative functions of the Environment Agency, strengthen the environmental divisions in other agencies, and prepare a comprehensive government system to handle global environmental issues." The final report emphasized the government as a whole, and there was not even a hint of anything about a "Ministry of the Environment." Why was the idea ignored in the report?

The primary reason is to be found in a fundamental shift in attitudes toward environmental issues that had occurred in the other agencies during the previous several years. When the Environment Agency was founded in 1971, such agencies as MITI, the Ministry of

Construction, the Ministry of Agriculture, Forestry, and Fisheries, and the Ministry of Transport which worked closely with the "sources of environmental pollution" had looked lightly upon the Environment Agency and environmental administration in general. However, in 1989, the so-called first year of global environmental awareness, the approach of those agencies to environmental issues had begun to change. For instance, the Ministry of Agriculture, Forestry, and Fisheries, the same agency that had built too many roads through farm country and installed irrigation systems damaging to the environment, proclaimed that "rice paddies and national forests are the foundation of environmental protection in Japan." MITI, which had been at odds with the Environmental Agency over such issues as the construction of electric power plants and other polluting industries, established a thirty-employee Environmental Policy Division within the Environmental Protection and Industrial Location Bureau and began speaking out on environmental protection. The Law to Encourage the Use of Recycled Resources, which took effect in 1991, was formulated mainly through MITI's initiative. MITI had rejected the Environment Agency's draft of a similar law, which MITI described as "all idealism and largely unfeasible."

When "global environmental issues" came up on the government agenda, agencies began asking for more money to address "environmental" concerns. "When the agencies ask for a budget, they cite 'environmental policy' for some items that seem hardly related to the environment," complains a high official at the Ministry of Finance's Budget Bureau. In the fiscal year 1992, of the total national budget allocated to global environmental protection, the Environment Agency was given 4.8 billion yen. Compare this to other agencies' shares: MITI received 130 billion yen for such environment-related activities as "technological development" and "cooperation with developing countries." The Ministry of Foreign Affairs got 7.5 billion yen for wooing the International Environmental Technology Center to set up its headquarters in Japan, among other things. The Ministry of Finance obtained 5.6 billion yen for financially supporting the development of environmentally related technology. The Ministry of Agriculture, Forestry, and Fisheries received 5 billion yen for combating acid rain damage to forests. The Ministry of Health and Welfare got 1.1 billion yen for investigating waste disposal measures. In budget making for the fiscal year 1990, three agencies asked for money for suspiciously similar sounding projects: the Environment Agency wanted money for a "Center for Global Environmental Research"; the Meteorological Agency of the Ministry of Transport wanted funds for a "Global Warming Information Center"; and MITI wanted a budget for an "Institute for Global Environmental Technology Research." (This kind of wasteful overlapping and interagency competition for funds abounds throughout Kasumigaseki.)

In 1989, when a Cabinet member was to be in charge of "global environmental issues," a long struggle had ensued over appointing the Environment Agency's director-general because of strong objections from the Ministry of Foreign Affairs and MITI. The bureaucracy's traditional territorial rivalries were affecting even environmental issues, and it was clear even then that the powerful agencies would never stand for a strengthened Environment Agency or anything like the establishment of a Ministry of the Environment, which would threaten their interests. What happened in late 1991, then, was that they lobbied the council so that it would refrain from mentioning the mere thought of a Ministry of Environment.

The relatively small and weak Environment Agency did not stand a chance. The Environment Agency was in no shape to lobby for ministry status. As a spin-off of the Ministry of Health and Welfare, the Environment Agency's power was severely limited from the start. In exchange for transferring its Air Quality and Nature Conservation divisions to the Environment Agency, the Ministry of Health and Welfare retained the authority to occupy the posts of administrative vice-minister, head of the Air Quality Bureau, and head of the Nature Conservation Bureau. The posts, along with chief of the Director-General's Secretariat, have always been reserved solely for Ministry of Health and Welfare bureaucrats. (Later, the administrative vice-minister post and the chief of the Planning and Coordination Division post came to be occupied alternately by bureaucrats from the Ministry of Finance.) Moreover, more than 50 percent of Environment Agency officials with rank above division chief are also

Ministry of Health and Welfare officials. Officials hired by the Environment Agency constitute little more than 20 percent of the posts.

The Ministry of Health and Welfare "welcomes an increase in the Environment Agency's budget, but not the broadening of its jurisdiction," stated a division chief at the Ministry of Health and Welfare. It is no wonder that the ministry's officials posted at the Environment Agency were indifferent to the Provisional Council's report. So were Environment Agency officials who came from other agencies. The Environment Agency has officials from up to twelve different agencies. This is another reason that the Environment Agency is no match for other powerful agencies. The highest-ranking officials hired by the Environment Agency are those recruited in 1972; they are still at the division chief level at best and then do not even head the most important divisions. It may take awhile before they assume the helm of the agency.

The LDP environment *zoku* legislators were the primary supporters of Nakamura's "Ministry of the Environment" idea. Environment *zoku* legislators such as Kosugi Takashi, Aoki Masahisa, Aichi Kazuo, and Takemura Masayoshi, and are the nucleus of the hot-shot group that spoke in favor of the LDP Policy Council's environmental division. (Later, both Aichi and Takemura left the LDP.) However, the environment *zoku* legislators were not totally unified. Former Environment Agency Director-General Kujiraoka Hyosuke, an environment *zoku* legislator and an influential figure in the LDP's environmental administration, stated: "I oppose the idea of a Ministry of the Environment. Some people may want to make the Environment Agency into a ministry in order to have the title of minister of the environment conferred upon themselves someday, but that would just be a silly, childish ego trip." Here is a summary of Kujiraoka's opposition. According to Kasumigaseki's procedures, to become a ministry an agency must control certain important tasks on its own. The only notable tasks that the Environment Agency seems to perform independently are the control and maintenance of the National Park System, which is not enough responsibility to upgrade that organization into a ministry. Consequently, the Environment Agency would have to take over responsibilities from the other agencies, including sewage and city parks, water supply maintenance and garbage disposal, and industrial waste disposal. Even if the Environment Agency were to assume some of those tasks and were to become a ministry , there would still be other problems. As things now stand, the agency has a "right to adjust policies" because it is an auxiliary organization of the Prime Minister's Office. But if it became a ministry it would lose that right. The establishment of a Ministry of the Environment would fragment, not unify, environmental policy, and it would create chaos.

The proposed Ministry of the Environment idea, which had apparently become a dead issue in late 1991, came back to life with strong political backing from an unexpected source. On February 6, 1992, at a Tokyo hotel, the LDP held the first meeting of the new "Conference on Environmental Issues" to thoroughly reevaluate environmental administration and consider means to strengthen it. Former Finance Minister Hashimoto was the conference chairman, and former Prime Ministers Takeshita and Kaifu (who quit the LDP and has become the president of the New Frontier Party) served as advisors. The eleven regular members of the conference included such prominent politicians as former LDP Policy Council Chairman Mitsuzuka Hiroshi, former Chief Cabinet Secretary Gotoda Masaharu, and former LDP Secretary-General Obuchi Keizo, all of whom were considered close to Takeshita. After the meeting, Hashimoto held a press conference. "Are you considering reorganizing the agencies through a change in environmental administration?" asked one reporter. Hashimoto replied, "If there were no need for change, we would not have held a conference like this," implying that he was resolved to proceed with the proposal to create a new ministry.

On March 16, 1992, Prime Minister Miyazawa Kiichi spoke to the Budget Committee of the House of Councillors of the Diet about the "Ministry of the Environment" issue: "We have to consider creating fundamental laws on the environment and think about what kind of system will be necessary." This remark was viewed as a sign that the prime minister also favored the conference's position. On May 11, 1992, the LDP released a draft of "Fundamental Laws on the

Environment," largely inspired by Hashimoto. It presented three main points:

1. Restructure the administration to unify environmental policy by such means as the creation of a Ministry of the Environment.
2. Consider necessary changes in fiscal, taxation, and financial policies, including the introduction of an "environment tax."
3. Establish laws requiring environmental impact assessment prior to the planning stage of commercial and industrial development projects.

As was anticipated, agencies that would be affected by the passing of the LDP draft put up an all-out opposition. With the support of industries, MITI opposed the environment tax. The Ministry of Construction, joined by MITI, opposed the environmental impact assessment. On October 20, 1992, the two government committees on the environment issued another draft of "Fundamental Laws on the Environment." This was a significantly weaker version than the earlier LDP draft on important items such as the "environment tax" and impact assessment. At about this time, the issue was waylaid when conference members, mostly from the LDP Takeshita faction, became deeply divided over the Kanemaru Shin corruption scandal. Kanemaru, probably the most influential manipulator in Japanese politics at the time, was Takeshita's benefactor. Bureaucrats believed that once the Takeshita faction settled its infighting, the conference members would regain momentum and there would be a lively debate on agency reorganization centered around environmental issues that would perhaps lead to further debate on restructuring all of the bureaucracy.

Which Agencies Will Survive?　What possible consequences do bureaucrats expect from reorganizing, merging, or abolishing agencies? Depending on which agency a bureaucrat works for or the year he entered the agency, there are many different opinions. For instance, a high official at MITI, where the new policy of partial alliances is being practiced, stated:

> I don't think the problems stemming from a vertical administration will be cured by forming stronger links among the agencies or giving more power to the prime minister's inner circle to adjust policies. The only solution would be either to let a Cabinet member select his own secretariat staff, as in France, or to make appointments of high officials subject to both executive selection and legislative confirmation, as in the United States.

On the other hand, many young bureaucrats advocate a new system in which government as a whole, not an individual agency, would recruit officials. Under the current system, the Examination for the National Civil Service is merely a qualification exam, or the first hurdle of many. Each agency then recruits its own new officials, administering interviews and other individual agency requirements or tests as has been described in the earlier chapters. Each agency might as well have separate bureaucratic entrance exams. The young bureaucrats' proposal would have the government as a whole hire all new officials and distribute them among the agencies according to actual demonstrable need. Those who advocate this also call for making interagency personnel transfers easier. At present, transfers are extremely difficult.

If personnel reform as described above can be enacted, the government may be able to adapt to changing needs without reorganizing the agencies. But whether a French or U.S. system would work in Japan is highly questionable. Moreover, the establishment of an extremely powerful personnel authority would be essential to recruit officials for all the government agencies. Even if the personnel authority were granted such broad powers, the outcome would still amount to a rehash of the current civil service examination system.

In any case, many other possible means of reforming Japan's government bureaucracy are presently being discussed: dismantle MITI; break up the Ministry of Finance; split up the Ministry of Posts and Telecommunications; bring back the pre-1945 Home Ministry. But all are merely ideas. What is actually happening now is something akin to the "survival of the fittest," as the agencies shrewdly prepare for reorganization. For instance, adjustment agencies such as the Environment Agency and the National Land Agency are viewed in Kasumigaseki as the most probable targets for "restructuring." High officials talk in private of the need to restructure such agencies as the Ministry of Foreign Affairs, the Ministry of Transport, and the Ministry of Education. In short, there is a consensus in the bureaucracy that the major agencies that are simply well-preserved vestiges of the "1941 system" have done their share of nurturing and promoting Japan's industries, but their heyday is long over. However, bureaucrats cannot reduce the size of the system by themselves, hence they focus their energy on recent urgent issues such as the environment or on criticizing the shortcomings of other agencies.

Powerful agencies such as the Ministry of Finance, MITI, the Ministry of Construction, the Ministry of Home Affairs, the Ministry of Health and Welfare, and the National Police Agency have started to use their institutional influence and expertise to reorganize Kasumigaseki. Consequently, interagency power struggles have become increasingly more complicated than ever. Some agencies have secretly formed a united front against the Ministry of Foreign Affairs. Meanwhile, MITI, the Ministry of Construction, and the Ministry of Home Affairs have formed a coalition to take on the rest of the bureaucracy. In conclusion, pending government reforms have led to an increase in the already intense competition among the powerful government agencies for influence, budget increases, and "colonies" within the bureaucracy.

POSTSCRIPT

How to Deal with Japanese Bureaucrats

Japan's bureaucratic system is organized both vertically and horizontally into an almost unbelievable number of divisions, with little cooperation among the different agencies. If foreign businesspeople and government officials feel that they are having a difficult time negotiating with Japanese bureaucrats, they should remember that the cause is not only because they are foreigners. Japanese people, too, are fed up with their own bureaucrats. Japanese journalists, even those with a lot of experience, find reporting on bureaucrats difficult, and Japanese businesspeople try to avoid having to deal with them.

The primary difficulty in reporting on bureaucrats is that they intensely dislike publicity. Even when a public relations film is created for their own agency, they refuse to take part if they have to reveal their names, claiming that in the group-oriented bureaucracy it is inappropriate for individual officials to be in the limelight. The real reason for their dislike of publicity is that publicity would make their colleagues look askance at them and it hurts their chances for moving up the career ladder. Not surprisingly, it is taboo for bureaucrats to appear on television or write books without the authorization of their agencies. Having a book published is normally considered an accomplishment, but in the bureaucracy such outside work is viewed as a waste of time and a sure sign that the author is shirking his or her official duties. It might even be considered a publicity stunt or an act of betrayal against the government.

Even when bureaucrats agree to be interviewed, they are extremely tight-lipped. They usually ask the reporter not to use their names or write in a way that might suggest the specific source of a remark. They only answer questions directly related to their own administrative jurisdiction, and if a question goes the least bit beyond it, they say, "I am not authorized to discuss that." Even when speaking about areas of administration that they are responsible for, if a question is related to some confidential matter or a scandal, the response "I will have to find out about that," is a common evasive tactic. They do not knowingly distort facts, but journalists must decide what to write and what not to write based on their interpretation of a bureaucrat's remark.

Bureaucrats also tend to be extremely proud and snobbish. If a reporter is not well informed on the present state of public administration or the topic in question, the bureaucrat being interviewed abruptly says, "I'm busy now. Please do your homework and come back later," refusing to answer any more questions. Bureaucrats can be formidable foes in the defense of their positions as well as in the defense of the bureaucracy itself.

These characteristics of bureaucrats are important for foreign journalists and foreign businesspersons to know, even though bureaucrats do tend to be a little kinder and gentler toward them. A high-ranking Ministry of Agriculture, Forestry, and Fisheries official explains:

> We bureaucrats tend to judge a person's importance in the first five minutes of meeting. If the person is Japanese, we can judge him or her by title and social status, and their appearance and behavior can be a further indication of intelligence. However, we don't know enough about foreigners, particularly Caucasians, to evaluate their importance by appearance and behavior alone because they live in a different social context. We normally decide how much detail to go into in a conversation depending on our judgment of a person's worth, but with foreigners it takes time to make that judgment. While making that judgment, we try to be polite to foreigners.

Let us suppose, then, that Japanese bureaucrats deal with foreigners and understand their "worth" and intelligence. Where do the bureaucrats go from there? A MITI official who just returned from a European assignment stated:

> There are foreigners who are really quite aggressive on a single issue. When we meet that sort of person, we try to see if they are interested only in a particular issue, or if they are people we will work with for a long time. If they are 'single-issue' people, we will shut the door on them in our minds. But if we can establish a long-term relationship with them, we try to be good associates. Luxurious Japanese restaurants don't welcome one-time customers, and we are the same way.

Japanese bureaucrats indeed become friendly and frank with others if they think these people are worthy of long-term relationships. Some bureaucrats also complain that Western-style negotiations are difficult for them to deal with. "In Japanese-style negotiations, progress is not necessarily made each time the interlocutors meet. In many cases, negotiators meet several times, establish confidence in each other, and then a breakthrough is made. But in the Western-style of negotiations, people expect progress each and every time we meet, and we don't know what to do," said a Ministry of Foreign Affairs official.

When dealing with Japanese bureaucrats it is useful to prove that one is worthy by their standards, and make them understand that one is intent on establishing a long-term relationship. When dealing with the maze that is the Japanese bureaucracy, there is no special advice that may be given other than the obvious tip that one must establish direct contact with the government officials of the relevant agency. For example, let us imagine that an American becomes good friends with a high-ranking Ministry of Foreign Affairs official at the Japanese embassy in Washington. Later he visits Kasumigaseki in Tokyo with a letter of introduction from this official, which he knows is necessary to gain an appointment. While the introduction would get him into the Ministry of Foreign Affairs, that American would be ignored at other agencies. Likewise, even if one had a strong contact at MITI, which, along with the Ministry of Foreign Affairs, handles negotiations on international trade, that would not be transferable to the Ministry of Agriculture, the Ministry of Health and Welfare, or the Ministry of Transport. One should also keep in mind that attempting to enlist an official from the one particular agency to act as an intermediary with another agency has the potential to backfire and provoke the second agency's hostility, thereby jeopardizing future talks.

As in the Motorola mobile phone incident, it is obviously useful to enlist a powerful politician who wields influence on a particular agency as an intermediary. Ozawa Ichiro, who practically ruled the Ministry of Posts and Telecommunications, may be a special case of this kind of influence; however, behind every agency there are politicians who influence decisions. For example, MITI Minister Hashimoto Ryutaro is influential in the Ministry of Health and Welfare, and Kajiyama Seiroku, former secretary-general of the LDP, has clout with MITI. On the other hand, even a prime minister or a head of the Prime Minister's Office may not be capable of wielding influence with an agency. Bureaucrats always keep a sharp eye on politics and know very well who has what amount of political power at a given time. Even a politician who does not hold a Cabinet post or an important position in the leading governing party of the time will find a receptive audience among the bureaucracy if has proved himself to be an able politician.

Another useful tip for the foreign businessperson is to obtain an introduction to an agency from an executive of a company that is supervised by that agency. Bureaucrats and business executives meet frequently and often have an ongoing relationship with each other. In some cases, you can get a bureaucrat who happens to be a college classmate of the bureaucrat you wish to meet to act as an intermediary. Even if they work for different agencies, bureaucrats are highly receptive to introductions from colleagues of the same graduating class. There is also a tight bond between same-year entrants to the bureaucracy.

Finally, the best way for a foreign businessperson to persuade a Japanese bureaucrat may be through reason. Japanese bureaucrats are an extremely proud, if not snobbish and exclusive lot, yet they tend to lend an ear to rational argument. To earn a bureaucrat's respect, one should carefully study the issues involved, prepare data and relevant information, and then engage in a debate with the bureaucrat. Losing the argument with the official would signal an end to discussion and any further contact, but if one can persuade the official in some way, the official will most likely give further thought to the issue.

The Japanese bureaucracy is no doubt a closed society. However, a foreign visitor who has succeeded in earning the trust of a high official may find it unexpectedly easy to blend in. The foreign businessperson should keep in mind that Japanese bureaucrats (with a few exceptions of those such as National Police Agency officials) tend to be more respectful and polite to foreign visitors than to Japanese visitors. Most bureaucrats are extremely afraid that a rude attitude on their part would reflect badly on Japan as a whole. Foreign businesspersons should note that a growing number of officials have experienced either study abroad or overseas assignment. In particular, all Ministry of Foreign Affairs officials have had overseas experience as have most MITI officials. Researching the cities and countries in which particular officials have lived could prove to be a valuable move, because officials usually love to talk about foreign places where they have lived.

A final point of advice is to remember that just as Japan's bureaucratic structure is strictly compartmentalized, so are the bureaucrats' attitudes, which split along agency lines and age groups. Also, there is often a great gap between the way the official bureaucratic organization works and what an individual bureaucrat thinks. While there are plenty of officials who want to maintain the status quo, most bureaucrats, including many MITI officials, believe that there is much room for reform, and such bureaucrats actually welcome foreign criticism.

A question that naturally arises as we end this book might be, why don't bureaucrats who recognize the need to reform practice what they preach? Japanese society is patiently waiting for an answer to this question.

INDEX